business
plan

business
plan

What to know and do to make the perfect plan

Kevan Williams

Prentice Hall
is an imprint of

Harlow, England • London • New York • Boston • San Francisco • Toronto • Sydney • Singapore • Hong Kong
Tokyo • Seoul • Taipei • New Delhi • Cape Town • Madrid • Mexico City • Amsterdam • Munich • Paris • Milan

PEARSON EDUCATION LIMITED

Edinburgh Gate
Harlow CM20 2JE
Tel: +44 (0)1279 623623
Fax: +44 (0)1279 431059
Website: www.pearsoned.co.uk

First published in Great Britain in 2011

© Pearson Education Limited 2011

The right of Kevan Williams to be identified as author of this work has been asserted by him in accordance with the Copyright, Designs and Patents Act 1988.

Pearson Education is not responsible for the content of third party internet sites.

ISBN: 978-0-273-74252-4

British Library Cataloguing-in-Publication Data
A catalogue record for this book is available from the British Library

Library of Congress Cataloging-in-Publication Data
Williams, Kevan.
  Brilliant business plan : what to know and do to make the perfect plan / Kevan Williams.
       p. cm.
  Includes index.
  ISBN 978-0-273-74252-4 (pbk.)
 1. Business planning. 2. Business writing. I. Title/
  HD30.28.W5437 2011
  658.4'01--dc22

                                        2010037453

ARP Impression 98

Typeset in 10/14 pt Plantin by 3
Printed in Great Britain by Clays Ltd, St Ives plc

To my wonderful wife Liz and wonderful children Rose, Dan and Sam for, as ever, their complete support. Must now be time for the beach ...

And to all of you who take the step and start your own business; congratulations and my very best wishes.

Contents

About the author

Having started as a driver's mate and factory hand in a pop (soft drink, not music) factory, I went through being an environmental radiochemist, researcher, food scientist, business development manager and trainer to find myself now a Director within Norwich Business School at the University of East Anglia and partner in a small research training and consultancy firm, Idiomplus. Alongside this I spent 19 years in part-time education from A-levels to PhD and MBA.

I've worked in the private, public and higher education sectors and have set up and run a small business. I hope I am able to see things from most sides.

Currently I greatly enjoy teaching postgraduate business students, mainly in the areas of strategy, marketing, change, leadership and working with organisations that are new to business ventures and business activities.

I have been fortunate to have had published one previous book, in 2009, a pocket guide to strategic management.

I live near Norwich, try to play golf, greatly enjoy car auctions and adore being near the sea.

Acknowledgements

It has been a privilege to be able to write this book and my heartfelt thanks go to Samantha Jackson at Pearson for believing in me and to Rachel Hayter for her willing support and words of encouragement.

Publisher's acknowledgements

We are grateful to the following for permission to reproduce copyright material:

Simon & Schuster, Inc. for the figure on p. 47. Adapted with the permission of The Free Press, a Division of Simon & Schuster, Inc., from *Competitive Advantage: Creating and Sustaining Superior Performance* by Michael E. Porter. Copyright © 1985, 1998 by Michael E. Porter. All rights reserved.

In some instances we have been unable to trace the owners of copyright material, and we would appreciate any information that would help us to do so.

CHAPTER 1

An introduction to writing your business plan

'Would you tell me, please, which way I ought to go from here?' said Alice.

'That depends a good deal on where you want to get to,' replied the Cat.

'I don't much care where,' said Alice.

'Then it doesn't much matter which way you go,' said the Cat.

Lewis Carroll, *Alice in Wonderland*

So we have our reason for writing a Business Plan; we need to be on the right road. We wouldn't start a journey without a road atlas so why would we start a business without a Business Plan? You will likely have any number of reasons why you want to start your business; money, dreams, opportunity, etc., but central to them all is wanting your business to be something, to achieve something, to go somewhere. No one starts a business wanting it to fail; no one wants to have all their efforts going to waste. We maximise our chances of success by spending some time thinking about our new business to ensure we set it out on the right road. This thinking about where we are going and the answers we find allow us to plan it right. That plan is our Business Plan.

Our purpose

First, our Business Plan needs to be convincing. In particular it must be clear to the reader that this Plan is describing a business that has an obvious and convincing purpose. In other words:

'What is the question to which my business is the answer?'

For example, within a large new housing development full of families and young people there is no fast-food take-away but there *is* an empty shop. To even the casual reader of the Plan it will be sufficiently clear that people increasingly enjoy take-away food and here is a need to which a proposed take-away business might be the solution.

Or the government may introduce new legislation that says all electrical equipment must be safety checked every five years. Who will do this testing? A new business?

Or new tax incentives encourage the production of energy from wind power. For individuals or companies who want to do this, who will they turn to for advice? Where will they go to buy wind turbines? Who will they pay to install their wind turbines? Here a new wind-power advice, supply and install business is the answer.

It is important to generate this initial interest in your Plan, for in doing so it will encourage the reader to examine it in more detail and to do so in a more positive frame of mind.

Next, your Plan must be capable of securing financial support. Of course not all business start-ups need this but most do, and even if yours doesn't, for your own sense of security it is a useful discipline to act as if you would be seeking others to support your business. (When it is our own business we can be overly optimistic and the Plan provides a useful check.) Financial support for a new business comes in many forms (covered more fully in Chapter 6):

- 'Soft money', e.g. loans, gifts from friends and family.
- Bank lending, e.g. overdraft, loan, credit cards, etc.
- Investor funding, shareholders, business angels, venture capitalists, etc.

All these people provide money to us on the basis that we will repay it along with some financial profit for them as a reward for providing us with the money. As such they need to know we will be able to repay it and in the beginning the only information they have to make this decision is from our Business Plan. So in addition to showing why the business needs to exist, the Business Plan must show how the business will make money and how much money it will make.

Finally, the Business Plan is for your benefit.

Reduce your plan to writing. The moment you complete this, you will have definitely given concrete form to the intangible desire.

Napoleon Hill, American author, 1883–1970

And this benefit comes in two ways:

- Arguably the most important is the process we go through in writing the Business Plan: the questions we ask ourselves and the answers we find forces us to think about the business in much greater detail and with a much more critical eye. It helps in turning our idea (or perhaps even our dream) into something based in reality; in doing so making it a better business.
- Then the Business Plan is our road map for the years ahead. As we run the business, especially in the early months, we need reassurance that we are on the right road. How do we know at three months old the business is doing ok? Well, we can look to see what our Business Plan said about where we would be in three months. If we are on target at three months it gives us some confidence that we

will be on target at six months, 12 months, etc. Whilst no guarantee, this is reassuring and gives us confidence that we are doing the right thing. If we are a lot under our three month Plan position, then the world isn't as we predicted and we must makes changes in what we are doing. And urgently! If we are way over Business Plan prediction (oh, what a wonderful position to be in), again we must make changes in what we are doing if we are going to keep up with how things are turning out.

> if the world isn't as we predicted we must makes changes in what we are doing

What are the readers looking for?

It depends upon who the reader is. Those of a financial background invariably 'look at the numbers'. In other words, they will look to see if the business will make money (see Chapter 5), e.g.:

- How much money will it make and how quickly?
- Does the business have good cash flow?
- How valuable will the business become?

Those considering investing in the business will be looking for similar financial dimensions but also will be looking at *you* and the management of the business, and whether you are up to the job, e.g.:

- Is there a clear opportunity/need for this business? What is the gap in the market that this business will fill?
- Do I believe the owner and/or the proposed management team have the capabilities to make this business work?
- How will I be able to get my money back? And how much will I get back?

A marketing person will invariably take a marketing perspective (see Chapter 4), e.g.:

- Where will this product/service fit into the market?
- Is the market sufficiently large or growing enough to enable the business to sell enough (and make sufficient money)?
- Can this business successfully build a brand?

Your family and friends are probably thinking,

- Is this business the right thing for you to do?
- Will it make you happy?
- Will we lose our house?

So in writing our Business Plan we must take into account all these factors because in reality it could be read by all these people. Satisfying all these individuals may seem a challenging task but by attending to a clear structure for the Plan (see later chapters) we will pick up all these factors along the way.

But there is one overriding issue here, and that is that our Business Plan must instil confidence in the mind of the reader. It has to be believable, it has got to make sense. So your plan must be well researched, it must be populated with facts and reasonable assumptions, and it must inspire their confidence in the business and in you. Again an apparently challenging task, but the structure here is designed to ensure this. The reason for this is that at the time of people reading your Plan, the business does not exist. They have nothing to go on in judging your business other than your Plan and arguably more importantly, they will be judging you. If they believe in you they are more likely to believe in your business. And part of you looking good here is that you have a well-considered and well-written Business Plan.

The structure of the Business Plan

All Business Plans tend to follow a similar structure. Any differences usually relate to the scale of the business and the scale of finances related to this. For example, if the business will be you alone making and selling craft items at craft fairs in the weeks leading up to Christmas, then the Business Plan is solely for your benefit in managing your business and can necessarily be on a modest scale, say a few pages. If you are launching a major property development business based upon securing £100m of start-up funding from investors, then the Business Plan by necessity has to be a substantial document that will become an investment prospectus for investors. The key is to match your Plan to the scale of the task it must address. A proposed structure is suggested below.

How to reduce your plan to two pages – the Executive Summary (Chapter 9)

- Writing a convincing Executive Summary.
- (We write it last but present it first.)

Getting started? (Chapter 2)

- What is the business?
- Describing what your business does.
- How does your business make money?

Competition – show how you'll beat them (Chapter 3)

- How to avoid competition.
- Giving your business a source of competitive advantage.
- How to analyse the future economy/industry/market.

Harnessing the power of marketing (Chapter 4)

- Using the power of strategic and promotional marketing (and how to avoid wasting money in marketing.)
- How to decide which customers you want – and which customers you don't want.
- How to calculate and set prices in the Business Plan.

Making money – the most important part of the plan! (Chapter 5)

- Understanding and managing income, costs, and profit.
- How to use the Business Plan to manage the cash flow.
- How to assess how strong your Business Plan is financially.

How you'll fund your business (Chapter 6)

- How to finance your business.
- Pluses and minuses of different options.
- How to approach people for funding and how to make the Business Plan attractive to them.

The people side of your plan (Chapter 7)

- Becoming the boss and how to manage people.
- Covering the different roles and procedures in managing your business, e.g. selling, production, delivery, etc.
- How to cover growing your business in the Business Plan.

Protecting your ideas (Chapter 8)

- Understanding the value of knowledge in a business.
- The role of knowledge in a good Business Plan.
- How to protect your knowledge.

One final area of differences between Business Plans is related to the type of business. All the sections above are usually there but the emphasis may be changed in some way. For example, planning for a shop, the emphasis will be on sources of competitive advantage, e.g. location. For a management consultancy business, the emphasis will be on knowledge and experience of the staff, so protecting what you know and people management becomes critical.

How to complete each section

This may be down to personal preference. Whilst all sections must be completed, the order and how they are put together will depend on you. Some people prefer to begin at section 1, line 1 and work their way through. Some will pick a section they think will be the easiest and start there, whilst others will write outlines or bullet points for all the sections and then go back and fill in the details. The key is that the Business Plan is actually written (and does not stay a dream!) and for you to do whatever works for you. The *how* doesn't really matter, but for each section there are two tasks:

- Gathering the information to help you write the section and
- Writing the section.

It is likely this will be an iterative process that leads to continuous improvement. For example, you may do some research into the market in your home town, write that section, then in writing it becomes apparent there may be a larger market in the neighbouring town so you will do more research and add to your Plan.

> it is likely this will be an iterative process that leads to continuous improvement

Don't be hung up on perfection. Yes, we must make the Plan as good as we can, and it must fulfil its basic functions of helping us plan and manage the business, but there is no such thing as a perfect Business Plan. Plus, a Plan is only ever a Plan, and once we implement it other factors may change, e.g. response of competitors, unexpected changes in the business environment, etc.

It is also important that we remember that a Business Plan is for life and not just for starting. Once you are up and running you will need to plan in more detail for the second year, etc., so there will be a need to create the next version and better information can be added into that.

The importance of the Executive Summary

For you, the Business Plan is your key tool in starting and managing your business. For others, e.g. bank staff (when you want an overdraft) or a business angel (when you want some investors), yours may be 'just another Business Plan' they have little time to read. Nearly everyone will want a summary of what is in your Business Plan so they can decide if they should consider it further. This is the job of the Executive Summary. It summarises all the key points of the Plan, e.g. what the business is, how it will make money, strength of its competitive advantage, etc. If they read this and its looks promising, they will probably read the remainder of your Business Plan. The Executive Summary needs the information from the main sections of the Plan so it is written last but presented first. Further attention is given to this in Chapter 9.

The scale of the task

As mentioned above, the approach to writing your Plan is a matter of personal preference. And the scale of the task will, as mentioned earlier, reflect the scale of your business. The craftware seller could write a sound Plan over the weekend if they are already familiar with the market. They will likely spread it out over time into three parts, e.g.:

1 Write the first draft, which will highlight the need for additional information.
2 Gather the information needed.
3 Complete Business Plan.

So, in all, it will be a few hours' work over a few days.

For the property developer example, this will likely involve talking with potential investors, funders, etc. and the writing of the Plan or here, particularly, the gathering of information, may take weeks to months. A project such as a revolutionary new internet business is on a large scale in that it changes how people buy products/services and redesigns the supply chain. It may take months or maybe even a year or more to achieve a viable Business Plan.

The scale of the task will also depend on the level of support you have. Will it be you alone or will you have knowledgeable friends or even advisors to help you? Undoubtedly a 'critical friend' or someone who will act in this role is an advantage in order to discuss ideas, help you in making decisions, etc. There are often government-funded agencies that will provide you with free courses on writing a Business Plan and/or provide an advisor to help you in this task. And of course you could pay a professional to help you. A good example here is an accountant. Yes, they will charge, but a couple of hours of their time (maybe £300 for a small local accountant who will probably be keen to win you as a new client) could prove very helpful and avoid costly mistakes. For example, they can check that your finances make sense, ensure everything is structured to minimise you tax liabilities and most will have a lot of experience of new businesses, and can guide you in the critical issues and signs to watch for.

For a more substantial business, e.g. the property developer example, you will almost certainly need a team of professional advisors, e.g. property experts, tax planners, financial advisors, management consultants, etc. Yes, it will cost you a lot of money, but nowhere near as much as a £100m mistake!

Finally, be aware of the time available. Of course the more time you spend on your Business Plan the more likely it is it will be improved, but you may not have a limitless period available. In the example at the beginning of this chapter, the empty shop and the potential fast-food business, that shop may not be available forever as other people may have also spotted the opportunity. So it is likely that writing your Business Plan will be a compromise of time needed and time available. And this may also help you avoid writing too much. If a Plan becomes too big it will inevitably mean the good points are lost in the words. Provided the Business Plan has sufficient of the main points to get people interested they can always ask you to provide more detail. Remember banks and investors are there to make money from you; they won't turn down a good business idea without asking you for more detail.

Preparing to write your Business Plan

Just start. For many people writing a business plan may be a daunting task, but as mentioned earlier, do not seek perfection. If you start you can always improve it as you go along. The world is full of people who say, 'I've always wanted to start my own business ...' or 'I've got this great idea for a business ...' Don't be one of those filled with regret, so don't let writing the Plan be the thing that stops you. Instead, make it the thing that starts you.

In preparation you will need:

- A Business Plan template (see the Appendix and later chapters).
- A way of writing it – a computer is best (it allows editing/ modification) but pen and paper is also fine.
- A folder to store it in – a ring binder is perfect as you can print out your draft Plan to put into the front of the ring binder and then the information/research you gather and use can be put into the back of the binder.
- Some background information/research is useful to start with but not essential (as you can fill this in as you go along).
- A 'critical friend' is very useful but not essential.

a 'critical friend' is very useful but not essential

● A deadline – a Business Plan is just a Plan until you put it
  into action and then you have a business.

In addition you will need 'information' to help you write your
Business Plan. Some of this you may already know, e.g., if you
are planning to leave your employer and start a consultancy in
the same business area. Other information you will need to find
and this is split into primary and secondary data:

● Primary – information you create yourself for this purpose,
  e.g. you interview some prospective customers, etc.

● Secondary – information already created and available
  somewhere, e.g. industry reports, newspaper articles, etc.

Some information is freely available and some you will need
to pay for. Be careful about accessing confidential information
and only do so if you have the right to do so. For example,
your current employer may have confidential market data it has
gathered and stored on its company network. But, and perhaps
frustratingly, you can only use this information if you have its
permission.

brilliant tip

Ssshhhh! Be careful and only show your Plan to trusted people.
You need to strike a balance between not giving away your ideas/
opportunities but being able to get feedback on parts of your Plan,
e.g. from potential customers.

Some sources of information include:

● Internet – either information created on the internet,
  for example on wikis, blogs, etc. or as the preferred
  publication channel for organisations, e.g. government
  departments. (Be cautious about internet material unless

it comes from trusted sources – anyone can create a web page.)

- Media, e.g. newspapers, television.
- Government offices, e.g. Office for National Statistics, international trade offices.
- Libraries.
- Large consultancy businesses, e.g. McKinsey, Tata Consultancy Services.
- Industry/trade reports, e.g. published by industry organisations themselves or by commercial research organisations.
- Academic journals.
- Potential customers.
- Potential suppliers.
- Trade associations.
- Network groups.
- Former employees/business owners that were in the industry/sector.
- Friends.
- Family.
- Etc.

brilliant recap

- Having a Business Plan makes sense because it helps you onto the right road. It will help you build a better business because of your having gone through the process of writing the Plan and answering the questions that arise.
- 'What is the question to which my business is the answer?' This is 'the point' as a business is only viable if it does something useful that is desired.

▷

- Think about the readers of your Business Plan and what they need to get from it.
- Make your own structure or follow the one given in this book.
- A Business Plan is never perfect and there is always an element of it being a work in progress. Never let the pressure of perfection stop you.

Start now ...

CHAPTER 2

Getting started

'This is our purpose: to make as meaningful as possible this life that has been bestowed upon us; to live in such a way that we may be proud of ourselves; to act in such a way that some part of us lives on.'

Oswald Spengler, German historian and philosopher

How to write Your Business Plan

Beginning here, Chapters 2 to 10 will guide you in writing your Business Plan. They will provide a structure based around Business Plan sections (highlighted by headings/sub-headings) that is duplicated in the Business Plan Template (in the Appendix). In addition these chapters and the Template include descriptions of the purpose of each section along with questions that will prompt you and help you in completing each one.

As mentioned earlier, you can finish the sections in what ever order suits you, e.g. sequentially or easiest sections first or … The order doesn't really matter but what *does* matter is that each section needs to be completed. Sometimes this will be straightforward; other times it will be a challenge when you realise you don't have the information you need. If this is the case, at the end of each section to be completed, add a small working table (as shown below).

To complete this section I need ...

Questions I need to answer?	What information do I need to answer these questions?	How can I find this information?
How many products do my two main competitors offer?	A product list for each.	Search their website or call them, posing as a potential customer (yes, I know it is a little naughty, but people do it!).
Which products should I prioritise?	Customer preferences.	Ask a few typical customers and/or call competitors.
Etc. ...		

What is my business?

This may seem obvious, but it is surprising how many business people stumble when asked this apparently simple question. Be clear. You want customers to give you money, so they need clarity from you as to why they should.

The first thing we write is a short, but complete, description of our business and where we want to take it. Having this clarity is vital for us in managing the business by giving us focus and clarity on what we need to do. For example, 'Helping people with computers as a business' is not wrong but it is difficult to manage this, to decide if it will be successful, attract customers (as it is too vague), etc., but if you say 'We will provide computer support to small businesses (up to ten staff) in my city', the proposition is much clearer. It is easier for you to decide what you need to do to get the business running and how to manage, and generally have a better idea of the direction you want to take. This is closely related to strategic marketing in Chapter 4.

This short description will not only be useful in your Business Plan but also when talking to people once you are looking for customers. You will bump into people all over the place and you will make arrangements to talk with specific potential customers. All will ask, '… so, what do you do?' And to sound convincing you need to provide them with a short, to the point statement containing what you do, and why they should use you. This short powerful statement can be derived once we have completed some of the sections within this part of the Business Plan.

 **action**

Write a short statement (say 30 words max.) that makes it clear what your business is and what it does.

Mission – or our reason for being

A business is hard work to start, to nurture and to make a success, therefore there has to be a fundamental reason for it to exist and for you to invest your time in it. Making money is obviously a good reason, but that goes without saying and isn't a good enough reason alone for the business to exist. There has to be more than that and making money, as important as it is, is therefore a by-product of your business.

> making money isn't a good enough reason alone for the business to exist

The reason your business exists we can call 'mission' and this can be summarised in your mission statement. Your mission has to include:

● The purpose of your business
● Why it needs to exist (this is about identifying the question to which your business is the answer)

- What it does (sells food, offers advice, supports disadvantaged people, etc)
- The values you believe in (and you will run your business by)

It has to appeal to all the stakeholders concerned with your business. Stakeholders are individuals and groups who have an interest in your business and how it is managed, e.g. shareholders, funders, customers, suppliers, trade unions, pressure groups, the media, etc. As they are interested in your business and can exert some influence/power over you, it is important we communicate with them and a mission statement is a succinct way of saying what we are about. Importantly, when we come to people (in Chapter 7), it can be a unifying and motivating force for your staff. And it may help you recruit staff.

In deciding your mission and in writing your mission statement it may help to look at those of existing companies and organisations:

Toyota – mission

'Toyota seeks to create a more prosperous society through automobile manufacturing.'

Google – mission

'To make the world's information universally accessible and useful.'

Tesco – mission

'Creating value for customers, to earn their lifetime loyalty.'

Oxfam – mission

'Oxfam International is an international group of independent non-governmental organizations dedicated to fighting poverty and related injustice around the world. The Oxfams work together internationally to achieve greater impact by their collective efforts.'

University of East Anglia – mission

'Our mission is to understand, empower and act, to enhance the lives of individuals and the prospects of communities in a rapidly changing world.'

Starbucks – mission

'Our mission: to inspire and nurture the human spirit – one person, one cup and one neighborhood at a time.'

So your mission statement should be relatively short, say one to three sentences, and can be quite challenging to write. But do not worry about it – just start writing it. Naturally, as you write other parts of the plan, your mission statement will be further defined. Just write something now … The examples below will help you on your way.

A new small building business targeting home improvements in its local area:

'Our job is to help local people make their home a nicer place to live. We will do this with honesty and we will never leave you to work on another job.'

A new outsourced office support business targeting small to medium businesses nationally:

'Our business works when your business works. We will be there when you need us to deal with those important tasks that need to be done and when time is money.'

⚡ brilliant action

Write your mission statement (say 30 words max.) that makes it clear what your purpose is.

Vision – where will you take your business?

'Mission' and 'Vision' may sound similar but they differ in the important element of time. Mission statements tend to be based more on the *now*, i.e. what we do and how we do it. Vision statements are focused in the *future* and are more about where we want to take the business.

Such a statement of future ambition is very important in the Business Plan because:

- It is an indication of the scale of our ambition.
- For funders, who will want to know when they will get back their money, the future of the business is very important.
- It is a future goal that we and our staff can work towards.

> your vision statement must describe the vision you have for the business and the future world

Important in writing your vision statement is that it must do as it says; it is a visual thing, it must describe the vision you have for the business and the future world, it must paint a picture of it.

 **example**

Avon – vision

The Avon Vision: to be the company that best understands and satisfies the product, service and self-fulfilment needs of women – globally.

Not uncommonly organisations' vision statements indicate wanting to be number one in their chosen market or industry.

One thing about both vision statements and mission statements, and something we need to avoid, is that they can become quite vague through the use of rather flowery language and sometimes through being designed by a committee. As a consequence, mission and vision statements went through a phase where people thought rather negatively about them. First, lots of statements came out saying, e.g. the business wanted to be the 'leading solutions provider' or 'make the world a better place', etc. What does a leading solutions provider do? What does it look like? What will it look like in the future? There is a genuine desire for mission and vision statements to be as inclusive as possible. An unintended consequence of this is that everyone has an input, the way to make it inclusive is to avoid excluding anyone, and very broad and general language needs to be used. Again this leads to a lack of clarity about what the organisation is about.

As a key part of the Business Plan we need to avoid this as we want it to be abundantly clear what we are about and what we want to be. Avon cosmetics above is a good example of not falling into that trap. They didn't say they wanted to understand people or understand everyone. Instead they said they want to understand 'women'. Very clear and immediately understandable. If the firm is this clear in its clarity of vision, then we can have increased confidence in the firm (and it encourages us to invest in them.)

Now write your vision statement. Again, don't worry about being perfect as you can modify/improve it as you go through the Business Plan process.

The examples below will help you.

For a new take-away business starting with one shop:

'To be the most recognised national chain of Chinese take-away restaurants in the UK by 2020.'

For a law firm:

'To be the foremost authority on international company law and international business transs.'

 **action**

Present your vision (say 30 words max.) that makes it clear what your purpose is.

Day-to-day activities

In the mission statement (above) you have set out the reason why your business needs to exist, including what it will do. And whilst it is very valuable to have these statements, the reader of our Business Plan will want to have a better handle on what we will actually do; in other words, translating the big picture into daily activities. Here in the Business Plan we have the opportunity to set out in more detail what you will do day-to-day for your customers, i.e. more specific information on what products/services you will offer.

So in the example of the new outsourced office support business, what will they do? Does this mean they answer your incoming telephone calls (a 'receptionist service')? Does this mean that clients telephone a call centre and the operator will then do what is needed, e.g. book appointments, produce a presentation, etc.? Or does it mean they will provide a named personal assistant to each client? And does that mean the p.a. works remotely, i.e. over the telephone or via email, or does it mean they will work at the client's premises from nine to five, five days a week?

In the Business Plan, again clarity is critical if our Business Plan is to be accepted and is to be useful to us. List the products and services giving as much detail as possible, e.g. as shown in the table below.

Chapter 3 provides more detail on products and services but they should be listed here in summary.

Product or Service	Target Customer	How made available
An outsource reception service that will answer calls, take messages, etc.	Small start-up tradesperson business that will not be able to afford a receptionist in their early days and risk missing customer calls when on jobs/driving.	Using a new telephone system that allows individual telephone numbers to be directed to the receptionist working in a small office.
A concierge-style p.a. service.	Self-employed international management consultants who need a p.a. available 24 hours to take account of international time differences.	A small team of internationally experienced high-level personal assistants working from an office in a large business centre in a major city.

 **action**

Present a summary of your day-to-day activities, particularly what you will do for customers and what you will do in your operations.

Your values and guiding Principles

Most people have values that guide them in how they run their business. And some are very well known, e.g. Anita Roddick at the Body Shop. Increasingly we see values (and guiding principles) more openly used in business and often referred to as a differentiator of a business from the competition, e.g. the Body Shop sold cosmetics as did many other firms, but it achieved advantage in the market through its stance against animal testing, supporting ethical positions, etc.

Some consumers, companies and public sector organisations do have views about issues like ethical trading, corporate responsibility, etc. and it affects their purchasing decisions. At the time of writing climate change and carbon emissions are very high

brilliant tip

Be aware that some (and only some) people who read your Business Plan may see business as about making money only and this 'values rubbish' as soft and fluffy nonsense. If you encounter such people, be sure to balance the values with money and highlight where they are a source of advantage in making money.

profile and purchasers are interested in low-carbon products and services. But this is only one issue and particular concerns of our times that have caused businesses to address their values and guiding principles include:

- The use of child labour in manufacturing.
- Deforestation.
- Inequality of wealth.
- The power of very large corporations.

Such issues are increasingly recognised in a formal way through 'triple bottom line' accounting. This model says that the traditional model of judging business by financial performance (only) is no longer adequate. We must therefore add a 'social' bottom line reflecting the impact of the firm on people and society, along with an 'environmental' bottom line that reflects the impact of the firm on the environment. This doesn't mean that we abandon profit, for without profit there is no sustainability, but that we take a more balanced approach to company performance.

> the traditional model of judging business by financial performance (only) is no longer adequate

Google is an example of a firm that has developed a set of guiding principles to help it manage its businesses.

 **example**

The Google guiding principles
As we keep looking towards the future, these core principles guide our actions.

1. Focus on the user and all else will follow.
2. It's best to do one thing really, really well.
3. Fast is better than slow.
4. Democracy on the web works.
5. You don't need to be at your desk to need an answer.
6. You can make money without doing evil.
7. There's always more information out there.
8. The need for information crosses all borders.
9. You can be serious without a suit.
10. Great just isn't good enough.

Update: We first wrote these '10 things' several years ago. From time to time we revisit this list to see if it still holds true. We hope it does – and you can hold us to that. (September 2009)

These guiding principles not only cover certain values but also help to define how the business will be run. This is useful information for investors/lenders and in helping to manage staff. And as a final part of describing our business, a set of guiding principles helps to define the culture of an organisation. Culture is an enormously powerful force within a business, for good and for bad, and it is helpful to establish the right sort of culture from the beginning. For example, will it be a risk-taking business? A culture that reinforces team or individual performance? A social or a financial perspective? Etc.

brilliant tip

Remember, how you run your business isn't only about your values and guiding principles but also about how your chosen customers feel about these issues; they are more likely to buy from you if they sense you are a kindred spirit.

brilliant action

You may wish to have a short statement on the values of your business. And then you may wish to define a set of guiding principles.

brilliant recap

- Be able to say in a few words what your business is about. A really great idea is easy to say.

- Create a strong sense of purpose as your mission. It will be a unifying force within the business and will be attractive to funders.

- The same group of people will buy into your having a strong sense of direction and where you want the business to get to.

- Remember, it cannot be all about the big picture and it is important to translate this into daily activities.

- Having values/principles by which you will lead and manage your business is a growing trend.

Competition – show how you'll beat them

The best victory is when the opponent surrenders of its own accord before there are any actual hostilities ... It is best to win without fighting.

Sun-tzu, *Chinese general and military strategist (c. 400 BC)*

 **impact**

Competition is bad because it leads to businesses being destroyed. Avoid it. Look for market opportunities with less competition.

Competitive advantage

Many people start their own business to pursue their dream. And this is a good thing. Indeed, if it is our dream it means we are more willing to stick at it, to get it going and to run it. However, and this is the bad news, just because we have a dream of running a business, it doesn't mean we have the right to do so successfully. This is nothing to do with legal rights or permissions or any other such factor, it is simply that a business can only exist if:

● It fulfils a need in the market; and
● It can do so better than its competitors.

Accordingly, two major parts of the Business Plan are concerned with the following:

- What evidence is there that a market exists for what my business will do?
- How can we achieve a source of competitive advantage within that market?

What is the need that my business will fulfil?

No business has a right to exist. In fact, one of the things of which we can be most certain is that all businesses will die (that is the second piece of bad news in two pages!). It is the role of management to keep the business going as long as it is feasible and worthwhile to do so. Therefore it helps if we have this in mind – my business has no right to exist and does so only as long as we are fulfilling a need and fulfilling that need better than anyone else.

How to give your business a source of competitive advantage

Consider that at some point in your life you have bought a pair of jeans (or other similar casual trousers). At the time you bought them, how many choices of retailer did you have? Were there local shops? Other shops in nearby towns/cities? Other shops in other countries? Mail order catalogues? Internet retailers? Others? It is likely you had maybe 50; or say you had 100 retail sources from which you could buy that pair of jeans. Yet you reached into your pocket, took out some of your hard earned money, and gave that money to only one of those retailers. That jeans retailer 'won' and the other 99 'lost'. That 'one' had a source of competitive advantage.

what will be the reason people will give their hard-earned money to you?

What will be *your* source of competitive advantage? What will be the reason people will give their hard-earned money to you and not to any of your competitors? This is a very important part of your business plan. And requires a significant part of your attention.

The famous management writer Michael Porter defined three major ways that a business can achieve competitive advantage.

1　Cost leadership – being lowest cost.

2　Differentiation – being better.

3　Focus – being specialist.

Cost leadership

 **definition**

Cost leadership
Competing on the basis of cost leadership is to be the lowest cost producer in the industry.

Cost leadership is about being the lowest cost producer in the industry. One point to clarify here is that lowest cost and lowest price are completely different. Setting a price will be discussed in Chapter 4, but to clarify here:

● Costs are how much it costs you to produce/deliver something.

● Price is what you charge your customers.

Say you are a baker; the 'cost' of producing a loaf of bread is made up of the cost of ingredients (flour, etc.), the cost of staff (to make the bread), the cost of equipment (mixer, ovens, etc.), the cost of premises (to accommodate the operation) and associated costs such as management costs, insurance, bank loans, marketing, etc. The 'price' is what you decide to charge your customers and is a reflection of marketing factors – position in the market, degree of competition, who your customers are, etc. (see Chapter 4).

 **impact**

There is no connection between the cost of production and the price you charge.

There is no connection between cost and price. Other than the obvious point that the price you can charge has to be higher than the cost of production.

But this example helps us see that if we have low costs we have more flexibility with our price. We can choose to charge a high price to attract a wealthy client base or we can choose to charge a low price to increase the volume of products we sell. We can choose to have sales and/or discounts and still make money. On the other hand, if we have high production costs, we have no option but to charge high prices and at times this may make us uncompetitive and we may not attract sales.

Some business markets are very price driven, i.e. a small difference in price will have a big difference in sales, e.g.:

- Markets where the product is similar to competitors' products, e.g. cheap, sliced, white bread.
- Markets targeting poorer people.
- Some business-to-business markets, e.g. restaurants buying basic ingredients (businesses tend to be less emotional when purchasing and focus more on price).

Within a low cost-strategy for your business there are two options:

- 'No-frills'.
- Low cost.

The former is an example of a business phrase that has entered everyday language in that we talk about 'no-frills airlines'. By 'no-frills' we mean the company offering products or services that are below the standard quality of the industry and consequently can be delivered at lower cost. For example, airplanes traditionally offered passengers coffee during the flight, no-frills airlines don't (or charge passengers for it). Traditional airlines allowed passengers to choose their seat before the flight, no-frills airlines don't. This doesn't mean that the products or services are of unacceptable quality, but rather that the quality is just acceptable for the target customer group.

Cost leadership is about providing products or services that are of comparable industry standard but at a lower cost. We achieve this in different ways but an example is having products of a standard nature made in a lower-cost country.

As part of your Business Plan, if you believe cost leadership (be it no-frills or low cost) is the right way for your business, then the key to success is for your whole focus to be on how you can continually cut costs. Everything about your business is about cutting costs, it becomes the culture of your enterprise so that you are always looking for and achieving cost reductions. The no-frills airlines are a good example of this. From their very beginning they challenged everything an airline does and sought to reduce the costs.

Some of the cost reductions tactics used by no-frills/low-cost airlines:

- They removed travel agents and asked passengers to call the airline direct to buy their tickets, saving the travel agents' commission.

- Then encouraged the customers to book their own ticket on the internet, saving the cost of their telephone ticket sales staff.

- Flew to smaller airports that were less busy – smaller, less busy airports have lower usage fees.
- Don't give refreshments to passengers – saving the cost of providing refreshments.
- Charge passengers for refreshments – turning a cost into an income/profit generator.
- Etc.

In your Business Plan, keep saying to yourself, 'How can we reduce the cost of this?' Success tips for cost leadership include:

- Economies of scale – e.g. your cost per unit of production usually reduces as you make more of something as you can buy your raw materials in larger volumes (at a bigger discount).
- Economies of scope – e.g. if you add a second product to your sales team's offer to customers then the cost of the sales team is halved.
- Low-cost design – e.g. we design products that satisfy the customers but are designed such that they are easy (therefore cheaper) to build.
- Low-cost manufacturing – e.g. have your goods made in a low-cost economy and then shipped to you.
- Low-cost staff – e.g. have some of your staff based in a low-cost country (either direct employees or outsource to a contractor).
- Low-cost location – e.g. do you need a building in the centre of the city (expensive) or could you be based in a more rural area (cheaper)? Note: we must be careful here for sometimes, e.g. in retail, hospitality or in clustered industries, location becomes critical and this can conflict with low cost.
- Being a smaller business – e.g. smaller firms do not need as many committees/meetings to run them.

● The use of technology, e.g. the internet to save on purchasing and marketing costs.

 **example**

Companies successfully using a cost leadership approach

● Ryanair – resource efficiency, taking out supply chain costs through removing travel agents, etc.

● Music CD sellers – by moving to countries with low tax regimes to avoid purchase taxes.

● Low-cost retailers in the UK, e.g. Aldi and Lidl, who save significant sums by reducing the number of products they stock compared to other supermarkets, e.g. stocking two brands of washing powder and not ten.

Of course, with any options for your business there will be downsides and this is so when following the cost leadership route.

● Just as there can only ever be one leader in a team, there can only be one 'cost leader'. Can you still be profitable if not 'the cost leader'? Yes, but it is a concern.

● Your cost leadership may be only a temporary advantage as competitors find new ways of reducing their costs.

● Cost leadership may not be so easy for a new business if other competitors have economies of scale, e.g. a large supermarket may be able to sell products cheaper than a small store can buy them.

● Continuous cost reduction can, at some point, go too far with the product/service eventually no longer of acceptable quality to customers.

● Chasing down costs can be a motivational game for some but for others it may eventually feel negative and thus impact upon staff morale.

Differentiation

 brilliant definition

Differentiation
Competing on the basis of offering products/services being better than the competitors. Being better has to be in a way that is valued by the customers and they must be willing to pay a premium price.

First, differentiation is about you being better than your competitors. Being better is obviously a vague description and exactly how you achieve it will depend upon your chosen customers (see Chapter 4), the industry, and on what basis you choose to compete. Examples include:

- A more convenient location, e.g. a shop in the right street/ neighbourhood.
- Higher quality service, e.g. dedicated telephone number to a named person, rather than to a call centre.
- A product of demonstrably better quality.
- A particularly strong brand.
- Particularly good personal customer relationships.
- A superior warranty.
- Superior customisation of the product /service.
- Faster delivery.
- More favourable payment terms
- Etc.

Next, differentiation is about being better in ways that your customers value. This is a particularly important aspect as it is the basis of charging a premium price. For example, there is no point in making your product available in ten colours (it will cost your more) if customers only want it in white. However, if your customers are worried about a technical and expensive product breaking down, offering a five-year warranty against everyone else providing a one-year will likely be a winner (and help you achieve competitive advantage).

It is worth noting that some people tend to assume that being better must be solely to do with the product. Not uncommonly, technical people such as engineers, scientists, etc. who are used to measuring things sometimes assume if the product is 3.2% more efficient everyone will buy it. Sometimes this isn't so and the best products don't always win. Sometimes it is the other dimensions of the purchasing experience, e.g. service, people and reputations, etc. that are the differentiation (although a better product as well will always help).

> the best products don't always win

▶ brilliant example

When first married and having bought a new house my wife and I needed to fill it with things. In the town, an independent electrical retailer offered '6 months' interest-free credit on anything over £50'. No formal agreements, no loans to apply for, just good old-fashioned credit where you went in and paid every month or gave them six post-dated cheques. Were their products any better? Maybe not, but their advice was better. Were their prices better? Frankly, I have no idea. But boy did we buy a lot of things there. They had worked out there was a good market in people like us who needed the products, were good for the money eventually but were cash poor. A good example of where differentiating may not be solely to do with your main products being better.

Finally, your customers' appreciation of the 'extras' offered by you must be sufficiently strong that they will reward you by paying you a premium price. By premium price we mean one that is higher than the industry standard. This follows a basic rule of pricing – if you are giving the customer something, they must give you something; in this case a price premium. A point worth emphasising is that the price premium (the amount above the market standard) must exceed the price it costs you to provide the differentiation services. For example, if you have a differentiated service by having faster delivery, it means you must keep larger stocks of product, so that costs you more. Continue to check that your price premium is covering your additional costs.

As before, with any possible approach there are downsides and for differentiation these include:

- The need to continually invest to keep being better is expensive – firms that differentiate often spend a lot on improving their products/services or developing new ones.

- Sources of differentiation may take time to develop.

- Sources of differentiation may change over time in customers' minds, e.g. what was once an extra now becomes the standard expected. For example, new car warranties used to be one year, then three years became the norm, and now some manufacturers are leading with five and seven years.

- Sources of differentiation may be more difficult to communicate. Cost leaders have a convenient headline figure called the 'price' they can use in communicating with the market/customers. How do we easily communicate that we have better customer relationships?

If you believe differentiation is for your business (and the promise of higher prices is always attractive!), then what is necessary? Important factors include the following:

- Do you have the wherewithal to be better?

- Do you know what the market values? And is willing to pay for?

● Do you have the enthusiasm and capabilities to keep ahead of the competitors?

 **example**

Companies successfully using a differentiation approach

● Waitrose – meeting the needs of a group of customers who are more interested in quality/choice, etc. than a low price.

● Apple – in making their products stand out, and in their case, stand out in many ways, e.g. design, ease of use, functions/applications and brand.

● BMW – by having a basic car and allowing customers to customise their vehicles by selecting options from an extensive options list.

Focus

 **definition**

Focus
Competing on the basis of being specialised and expert in a relatively narrow range of activities and offering to a small part of the market.

Focus is about being a specialist. It is about choosing to be exceptionally good at a little (rather than being just good at a lot). It is a deliberate choice, just like cost leadership and differentiation, but it is also often the default choice for starting a new business. In the beginning we often don't have the money to do a lot, so focus on doing a little. Also, people leaving their job and starting their own business often start in their area of experience and expertise and 'focus' on what they know best. (As the business grows they can afford to employ other people to widen the scope of what they do.)

The basis for competing with a focus strategy includes the following:

- Exploiting your (and your colleagues') in-depth knowledge.
- Possibly you already have a reputation in this area (based on your previous employment).
- It can be cheaper to start in a small area.
- There may be less competition – big firms need big markets so they frequently leave smaller 'niche' markets available for others.
- These niches markets, with little competition and requiring specialist knowledge, can be very profitable and it is easy for a small company to dominate a niche.

▶ brilliant example

Companies successfully using a focus approach

- Porsche – its core business is designing superior performance, two-seater sports cars.
- Linn – precision engineered music systems.
- Your local wine shops – the big supermarkets can only stock mass-produced wine as small vineyards cannot produce sufficient volume for them, so there is space for independent experts to sell wine from smaller vineyards.

❓ brilliant questions and answers

Look at the businesses you use, e.g. shops, internet retailers, tradespeople, and decide how they are competing: cost leadership, differentiation, focus, or some combination of these? Which of these businesses do you predict will do well?

 **example**

Achieving competitive advantage in the car industry

Approach	Examples	Basis of Competition
Cost leadership	Kia, Tata, Proton	Lower-cost production countries. Tending to be second-line in technology so reducing R&D costs. Standardised cars (everything is included, no options) leading to cheaper production costs.
Differentiation	Mercedes-Benz, BMW, Audi	Making cars to customer order. Selling exclusivity by your car being unique (the opposite of standardised). Investing in R&D to keep a flow of new technology.
Focus	Porsche	Doing one thing well (for Porsche, high performance, two-seater sports cars). Becoming recognised in the industry and the market as expert in this area. Continuous investment to always become more expert.

Which one is the winner?

Choosing the right strategy is dependent upon answering a number of questions:

- What does the market want?
- Which markets look attractive in the future?
- Where are the gaps in the market (i.e. no competitors)?
- Which type of strategy do you want to pursue for your business?

● Where could you build and achieve sustainable competitive advantage?

the winning approach will be a case of balancing your internal desires with what the market wants

The choice of the winning approach will be, as is usual, a case of balancing your internal desires with what the market wants.

In any market there are usually companies pursuing each of the competitive advantage strategies, but there are often gaps. In the 1990s there was a tendency for UK supermarkets to be more mid- to higher-end (quality focused) and less lower to middle end (value focused). This left space for Asda to refocus, for Morrisons to become a national business in this area, and for the continental European retailers, e.g. Aldi and Lidl, to enter the UK market in the lower to middle end. As the UK economy entered the credit crunch/recession these firms were well placed to benefit from a shift towards more value-focused shopping. And with cuts to public sector spending probably impacting consumer spending over the next few years, these value-focused retailers are set to continue to do well.

Of course, seeing a market is only part of the equation and our business has to develop systems to be able to exploit this opportunity. For example, for the value supermarkets, they have to have efficient and low-cost systems that help them in serving a high number of customers per day/per hour to maintain throughput. (If we are to make money in value systems, we need a large number of customers.)

So, in choosing which way to operate, we need to analyse the market by plotting where each competitor fits into it (see figure below). It is not easy to do this precisely but do what research you can by using your judgment, asking people their opinions and analysing competitor prices as a means of positioning (e.g. leaders low-cost, etc.).

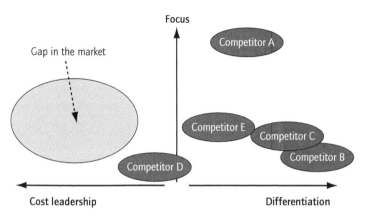

From Porter, Michael E., *Competitive Advantage: Creating and Sustaining Superior Performance* (The Free Press, Simon & Schuster © 1985, 1998 Michael E. Porter)

Why do we look for a gap? In short, because there is no competition there so we can have a bigger impact. Of course, we do have to assure ourselves that there is a market there. If we go into a market or part of a market with a lot of competition then we have a fight and it will be more difficult for us. Our only other option in a competitive market is to become stronger than the existing competitors, hopefully put them out of business and eventually come to dominate the market or our part of it. This is a viable plan but it takes more time, money and effort than finding and developing an uncontested part of the market.

 **action**

Which of the generic strategies will you pursue (one paragraph)?

Explain why you are making this choice (two to three paragraphs).

Map yourself and your competitors on the basis of their competitive strategy (cost leader, differentiation, focus.)

It's all about sustainability ... and not the green type

If our business does well it will attract attention from others, including our competitors, and those who are considering starting a business. If we are making money, others will soon see it and want a piece of our action. So how do we repel them? Options include:

- First-mover advantage – if we are in first, develop our products first and build a reputation (brand) then we are leading and others have to play catch-up. So we develop a product (that takes some time), launch it, sell it, win market share, etc. and by the time our competitors have entered with their product, we have already won the customers against no competition). And the competitors now have a contested fight to win the customers against us. Also by the time they have launched their product, we've had time to develop a new version of our product. (If this sounds a very attractive option it is tempered by the first-moving having more of the market development costs and risk.)

- Build a reputation (brand) – that period of uncontested operations is the chance to develop a presence in the market such that you continue to dominate even as other competitors enter. It is even an opportunity to build the company or product to become the generic name (or synonym) for a class of products, e.g. Hoover for vacuum cleaner, Sellotape for sticky tape, Tannoy for public address system. Or sometimes, even a new verb; 'to Google' for 'to search'. There may be some complications for trade marks here (see Chapter 8) but it can help the sustainability of our business.

- Develop some unique fit about our products to ensure customers remain with us. When we have more than one product, we can make our products work together in particularly efficient ways and thus our customers are likely to buy more and remain loyal to us. And because they want/need to buy from us, it makes it difficult for others to enter the market. Plus, it can lead to premium prices. A good example of this is Apple.

 **action**

How will you build sustainability (business, not green) into your business plan? Spend two to three paragraphs explaining how you will stay ahead of your competitors and why your business will have a future.

Analysing the future world

'The future belongs to those who prepare for it today.'

Malcolm X, *US black nationalist leader (1925–1965)*

If the opportunity is *now* we want to be quick off the mark with our Business Plan and getting the business up and running. But our Business Plan is really about the future. Therefore we must be able to predict the future and ensure our business is best placed for the future world.

> we must be able to predict the future and ensure our business is best placed for the future world

Fortunately we have some easy-to-use analytical tools to help us here:

- PESTLE – helps us understand the changes in the big things in life, e.g. economies, politics, etc.
- Porter's 5 Forces – help us understand the forces that are occurring within a single industry.
- SWOT – helps us to compare the relative performance of our business with the issues occurring in the business environment/industry.

Doing a PESTLE analysis

PESTLE stands for Political, Economic, Social, Technological, Legal and Environmental – the macroeconomic forces that shape our world. These are big, even bigger than the biggest firms, so are not things we as an individual business can change. But we can predict them and manage around them.

PESTLE factors are:

Political	In general things done by government, e.g. new laws, changes of laws, issuing policy statements, political ideology, etc.
Economic	Performance of economies, lending policies, stock markets, exchange rates, interest rates etc.
Social	Changes in population and population structures, beliefs of society, changes in what is and isn't acceptable, etc.
Technological	Developments in technology that change the way the world works. New technologies make some things obsolete and other things possible. The big technological change of our times is the internet, but there are others.
Legal	Overlap with 'Political', but here we might include specific laws, e.g. pollution laws, or those specific to business, e.g. employment regulations for younger workers.
Environmental	Issues both legal and social around the environment and its protection, e.g. waste disposals, what is no longer acceptable, etc. The big issue of our times under this heading is climate change, the role of 'carbon' and therefore carbon issues.

You might also see PEST or STEP – these are the same analytical tool but they do not include the Legal and Environmental factors.

As an individual business we cannot stop or change macroeconomic factors, but what we can do is look for them, predict them and make decisions that ensure our business is in as good a position as possible to deal with them, as follows:

● We need to have mechanisms in place to 'scan the environment' to look out for those economic factors that may impact our business.

● We need to assess the likely impact of these things.

● We need to develop solutions for our company to negate the issue or develop solutions to get around the problem or develop solutions that exploit opportunities presented by the predicted factors.

For example, a national recession is an 'Economic' factor. It isn't something we as a business can stop, but we can do some things to address its impact, outlined in the box below.

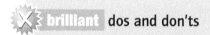 **brilliant** **dos and don'ts**

Do

✔ Have a system for watching what is happening in the world and collating this information within the business.

✔ See this as an opportunity to develop opportunities.

✔ Try and spot signs early to give your business a competitive advantage.

Don't

✘ Be too focused on today's crisis in the business.

✘ Think these are too large to be connected to your business.

✘ Just read about it in the media, as useful as that is, because competitors might be reading the same articles – you want to spot these things *before* your competitors.

 **tip**

On doing the PESTLE

- This is research and it is never possible to do a perfect PESTLE; just do as much as you can.

- Numbers make a big difference, i.e. saying 'the population is ageing' is helpful but saying, 'the population of older people will increase by 25%, 3,000,000 more, by 2020 is more helpful.

- We are probably looking to find approximately five or six major items under each heading but it can be more or fewer.

- If unsure whether something should be included, best put it in and then re-evaluate later.

- Sometimes it is difficult to know under which heading to put an item, e.g. is government increasing taxation to fill a budget deficit a political issue or an economic issue? It doesn't really matter; the key thing is to have it in our PESTLE.

brilliant timesaver

A PESTLE is not about your business, nor even your market: it is about the big things happening in the world. We use this analysis to identify what the future will be like. Once we have a sense of this future world, it gives us insights into what our business needs to be doing in the future.

 **action**

Present a summary of your PESTLE analysis to highlight the key issues that, in the future, will provide opportunities for your business and that will be threats to your business.

Include a copy of your full PESTLE analysis in the appendices to your Business Plan.

Doing Porter's 5 Forces analysis

PESTLE looks at the big things and these affect all industries, e.g. a change in national interest rate policy will impact upon the domestic housing market and the business consultancy market. But each of these markets will likely be affected to different degrees – interests rate changes, for example, tend to have direct impacts on housing but perhaps less so on business consulting. It is therefore important that in analysing the future world we seek to also understand our chosen industry or market, e.g. local takeaway food, wind-power industry, etc, in more detail.

A useful tool to look at a specific industry is Porter's 5 Forces (P5F). This looks at, not unsurprisingly, five forces that we see operating in an industry (or market) and it gives us a sense of how easy it will be to operate successfully in this market. Here we are seeking to understand the forces that will impact upon our business (this time from within our industry) and do so by gathering information to ensure we position our business in a good industry/market where competitive forces are not too strong and where we can make good profits.

Porter's 5 forces are:

Potential entrants: How easy is it to enter the industry/market? If it is easy, we can readily enter the market, but so can others, so if we do a good job, this will attract others and our advantage may not be sustainable. Sometimes, it may even be more attractive to invest in entering a more difficult to enter market as once we are there and successful, others will be less able to follow (so strengthening our competitive advantage).

Potential substitutes: Can your product/service be readily replaced? This is not only about direct competitors but about new ways of achieving the same thing. For example, CDs were used to store data, and if we made CDs we competed with other CD manufacturers, but then along came USB memory devices … and data CDs were substituted.

Power of suppliers: This, and power of buyers, is about relative power. Do we have it? Or do others have it? We always want it! To make our product we need a particular raw material and there is only one supplier of it – who has power? Answer: the supplier, because they set the price we have to pay, they determine if us or our competitors get the supplies. In effect another firm has too much power over us and we will not like it. So this make it an unattractive industry to enter.

Power of buyers: The flip side of this is who is more powerful, us or our customers? If we run a bar, how easy is it for our customers to start using another bar? If it is easy for customers to switch, that is less attractive to us. If our customers are in some way tied into us (e.g. software suppliers) this is more attractive.

Competitive rivalry: How many competitors are there or will there be? Remember competition destroys businesses so more competition is less attractive (unless we are the destroyer!). A growing market in general can sustain more competition, but a shrinking market means that some businesses must leave or fail.

On doing the Porter's Five Forces

...similar to doing a PESTLE, it is research and so never perfect. Do the best you can, focus on the what you believe to be the key issues, don't worry about under which heading something fits (just put it in somewhere) and keep the P5F under review.

✦ brilliant action

Present a summary of your Porter's 5 Forces analysis to highlight that it shows the (current and future) degree of competition in your chosen industry/market, and what factors make it attractive for your business to enter.

Include a copy of your full P5F in the appendices to your Business Plan.

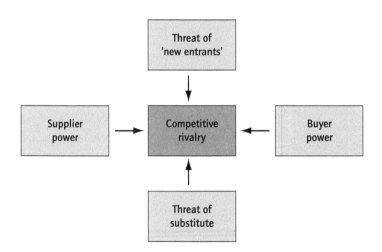

SWOT analysis

PESTLE and Porter's 5 Forces (P5F) analysis both look at the external world, which is good, as to be successful our Business Plan must be grounded in the reality of the marketplace. However, we also need to link the external and the internal dimensions and a SWOT analysis is a useful way of doing this (see figure above).

Like the PESTLE and P5F, with the SWOT we spend time looking at ourselves and the external environment to identify the things that we should be concerned about.

Strengths	These are areas where we are strong as a business (or planned business). By definition they tend to be internal factors. Examples include: good brand/reputation, good locations, strong management team, large cash-pile, etc.
Weaknesses	Again internally focused. Examples include: staff recruitment problems, too much debt, etc.
Opportunities	These are externally focused and represent the opportunities in the external environment. Here we can draw on the research from our PESTLE and P5F. It presents the opportunities that our business could develop/ follow. Examples include: new legislation that provides a new market, a potential competitor withdrawing from the market, the opportunity to buy a good brand established in the market.
Threats	These are the things to worry about. Threats have the potential to end our fledgling business or to bring our established business to a halt. Examples include: new legislation that takes away our market, an international competitor entering our market, a new road rerouting traffic away from our premises.

	Positive	Negative
Internal	Strengths	Weaknesses
External	Opportunities	Threats

brilliant recap

- Your business will only survive if it has a source of competitive advantage. There has to be something that causes your chosen customers to give you their money and not one of your competitors.

- Further, your source of competitive advantage must be sustainable.

- Competition is broadly assessed on the basis of being lowest cost, being better or being specialist. Each has certain factors that you need to achieve to be successful.

- It is important to analyse the world now and look for trends that enable you to paint a picture of what the future will be like. Your task is to develop your business so that it can be successful in that future world.

- Remember, competition is a destructive force and will kill your business; avoid it if at all possible.

CHAPTER 4

Harnessing the power of marketing

'The market is not an invention of capitalism. It has existed for centuries. It is an invention of civilization.'

Mikhail Gorbachev, *8 June 1990*

Marketing – the key success factor

Make no mistake, marketing has the power to make or break your business. Some regard marketing as 'spin' or hype. Some regard it as just advertising. And some see it as the ultimate way of wasting money. Yet it is oh, so much more than any of these; get it right and it will make your business.

⚡ brilliant questions and answers

Ⓠ Think and list some successful companies you use and/or admire.

Ⓐ BMW, Apple, Chanel …

What does this tell us? First, that they make good products, but other companies also make good products, and we've not heard of those companies. What separates out the successful companies? Marketing. They recognise a good product isn't sufficient for success; it has to be marketed successfully.

'Now we understand that the most important thing we do is market the product. We've come around to saying that Nike is a marketing-oriented company, and the product is our most important marketing tool.'

Phil Knight, CEO Nike

brilliant definition

Marketing
The process of deciding the customers you want and the customers you don't want and communicating effectively to both groups.

How to avoid wasting money in marketing

Occasionally you will meet people who tell you marketing is a waste of money and it doesn't work (often the same individuals tell you it is unfair people don't support businesses like theirs …). Invariably those with little faith in marketing have come to this conclusion because they once did some advertising and it didn't get them a single customer. Their first mistake was to confuse marketing and advertising – they're not the same. Secondly, they failed to appreciate the difference between strategic marketing and promotional marketing.

brilliant timesaver

Take time to understand the differences between strategic marketing and promotional marketing and use this knowledge in planning your marketing; you will save a fortune!

 **definition**

Strategic marketing
Deciding what you want to do, which markets you want to be in, which customers you want, who your customers will be, how you will position your products in the market, your core messages, etc.

Promotional marketing
Simply communicating these messages to your chosen customers, e.g. advertising.

It's like building a house. Strategic marketing is the foundations of the house. Get the foundations right and the remainder of the house has the chance to be good. But if your foundations are poor, you can throw as much money at gold taps, plasma TVs and the like as you want but it will still be a poor house.

Most businesspeople who do not believe in marketing, when they do try it, mistakenly jump in and do some advertising (promotional) without doing the strategic marketing. A fantastic way of wasting money. A colleague once visited a small business owner who was very angry that he'd done some marketing and it was a waste of money. It turns out that he had met an advertising salesperson who had sold him a radio advertising campaign – several thousand pounds. My colleague asked him if any of his potential customers listen to this particular radio station? 'How am I supposed to know that?' he asked. A classic case of throwing money at advertising without planning the marketing first.

There is no shortage of advertising salespeople who will call you all the time and they will all have very positive figures to prove what they are selling will work. We never deny another business person the opportunity to make a profit but let them make a profit out of other people. Our role is to decide our marketing strategy and then we call them to make the right things happen.

 **action**

Present your

(i) strategic marketing and

(ii) promotional marketing plans.

Marketing and sales

As seen above, marketing (and specifically strategic marketing) is about making the big decisions – which customers, offering, pricing, etc. – and then this is communicated to the market via promotional marketing. Some of this promotional marketing will be done electronically (e.g. website) and some in writing (e.g. newspaper adverts), but some in person. And this person-to-person communication part of marketing is what we call 'sales'. Sometimes we meet organisations that regard marketing and sales almost as separate things (actually usually the same firms that think marketing is just advertising) but they are wrong: sales is part of marketing.

It is worth highlighting here that if we have no marketing and no selling, we will sell nothing and very quickly go out of business. Now we may have a stereotype of a salesperson – perhaps as someone in a suit with a PowerPoint presentation or someone in a shop who pushes products at you – but it doesn't have to be this way. As a business owner we should always be talking to people about what we do – this is selling.

Later in this section we will look at the selling of 'services' and in that case the *person* who is selling is everything.

Having said sales are very important, there is a situation where you
may not need salespeople. If your
marketing is very good, and here
we mean *very good*, you can create
such a demand that customers come
to you. Think about the latest elec-

> as a business owner
> we should always be
> talking to people about
> what we do – this is
> selling

tronic gadget or the latest designer handbag. The companies
behind them are so good that they use the media and other
communications to release news items, snippets of information,
etc. that creates such a desire customers rush to the shops to
buy. In fact sometimes this is so good, and supply is deliberately
restricted, that customers have to go to the shop to put themselves on a waiting list to have the privilege to buy the product.
In this case you don't need salespeople in the shops, you just
need charming order takers.

 **action**

Summarise your marketing and sales activity.

I need a Lexus ... a big expensive one

It is true that I am often heard to say, 'I need a Lexus.' Or I hear
others say, 'I need that ... handbag', 'I need that ... phone.' My
family quite rightly point out that I don't need a Lexus, but that
I 'want' a Lexus. As much as I argue, they are of course right and
this illustrates a key point in marketing, and in the reason our
business exists (Chapter 3). 'Needs' and 'wants' are different.

A 'need' is a fundamental thing. A good example is hunger.
When hungry, we must eat. Otherwise we will, ultimately, die.
Other basic needs are warmth, shelter and love (less easy to

buy). It therefore becomes clear that those who fulfil a 'need' have a strong potential business.

A 'want' is a need with more choice. For example, if you have to walk and have no shoes, you will buy any pair of shoes. If you already have shoes you may then 'want' a particularly brand of shoe. Likely this choice will be influenced by marketing, the opinion of friends/other people, etc. Whilst less fundamental than a need, a 'want' can still be very powerful. However, no one ever died because of having the wrong brand of shoes so wants may be less powerful in driving customers to purchase.

At the time of writing many countries have been or are in economic recession. With people being or feeling poorer they have still spent money on food (a need) but replacing their aged, worn but still functional dining table? Well, that is a 'want' and that can wait until people start to feel wealthier again. Hence food retailers are still doing ok but furniture retailers are having a difficult time.

However, be it a 'need' or a 'want', neither is of any use to you unless the prospective customer has the money to buy what you are offering.

'A customer is not a customer until their money is in your bank account.'

Anon.

 **action**

Write very clearly and precisely the 'want' or 'need' your business is addressing.

Products or services

The things we sell fall into two categories: products or services.

 **definition**

A product
'Anything that can be offered to a market for attention, acquisition, use or consumption that might satisfy a want or need. It includes physical objects, services, persons, places, organisations and ideas.' Kotler *et al.*

A service
'Activities, benefits or satisfactions offered for sale that are essentially intangible and do not result in the ownership of anything.' Kotler *et al.*

Products and services are different and the distinction between them is vital in our planning for two reasons. First, services are usually more profitable and secondly, deciding if you are a product or service business is important because it requires different marketing approaches.

Products are usually less profitable for the reason of lacking a strong sense of competitive advantage. Consider the situation where you buy products and then resell them (a common retailer or distributor situation). The problem here is that other people will be selling the same thing (unless you can get an exclusive distribution agreement – then you have a competitive advantage!). And they will probably be attempting to sell the same thing at the manufacturers' suggested retail price so customers now have the choice of buying the same thing from two retailers. Multiply that by ten and the customer has lots of choice but any one retailer lacks a source of competitive advantage. If this is a growing market, everyone can sell and make a living. If it isn't growing, how does one retailer win over the other? The customer can compare you so has all the power. Likely they will call a competitor and ask for a price reduction to buy from them. Then they will call a third and see if they can get the price even lower. From our perspective as a business owner this is bad as it is driving down prices and pushing us toward a loss. The issue is that there is no difference between the competitors other than price. So presumably the customer will buy from the retailer of lowest price. With each customer calling this ongoing pressure eventually drives prices lower and lower until eventually products are sold at cost and we have no viable market.

This is a slight simplification because you can do things like spend more on marketing, use your brand to try and win, be more friendly, have your shop in a better location, etc., but the fact remains that if you are all selling the same things, competitive advantage is harder to achieve.

With services, what the customer is buying is dependent upon who is delivering the services. As this is dependent upon staff, and all firms have different staff, the service is unique. Therefore it is much more difficult for customers to compare prices as they are in effect comparing 'apples with pears'. By making direct comparison more difficult, the customers are less focused on price comparisons and will be more focused on other aspects that we highlight in the marketing. In general we prefer them to make purchasing decisions not on price, and as such prices can usually be higher, in turn leading to higher profits.

The big changing force in the shift from product to service has been the internet. In the past when you wanted to buy a washing machine you usually went to your local electrical retailer. Now a very significant number of consumers will log on to the internet to identify the recommended washing machines and then once a machine has been selected, use price comparison websites to find the lowest price. Likely the lowest price will come from an internet-based retailer as normally they have a lower cost base. For example, selling washing machines on the high street is expensive as rents there are costly anyway and washing machines take a lot of storage space. As the internet retailer has its shop window on the internet, it can put its washing machine into cheap storage facilities away from the high street.

So if the internet seller of products will always be cheapest, how can a retailer compete against this? By moving away from selling products towards selling a service. In reality most customers, and I use myself as an example here, don't want to buy a washing machine; they actually want to buy a means of doing their washing. They don't want a washing machine to be delivered to their home; they want someone to deliver and install a washing machine so it is up and running, and to take away the old machine. Also they want the reassurance that if their new machine goes wrong, they can call the local retailer who supplied it, who knows what they are taking about and will pop round and fix it. The local retailer has successfully moved from being a 'box-shifter to now providing a service. They have realised that for their customer an easier life is more important than an absolute lowest price product that could be obtained from other places.

> the local retailer has successfully moved from being a 'box-shifter to now providing a service

And now it is more difficult for the customer to make price comparisons as they are comparing a product with a service. Plus the service includes a 'convenience factor' for which the customer will reward the service provider with a price premium.

This is not to say one cannot make money selling products. Of course more specialised product providers will have fewer competitors and the price reduction pressure will be lessened. And in a growing market, where product may be in short supply, again there will be no price reduction pressure, e.g. think of the latest smartphone; in demand and everyone sells it at the same high prices.

So we have a choice:

- Sell products – against internet retailers.
- Sell services – with potentially higher margins.
- Sell products via the internet – with its lower cost base.

 **action**

Consider and state what products you will sell. If products, make some comment on how you will maintain the price margins vs internet retailers. Or become an internet retailer. Or say how you will move your products to become a service. Or if you will sell a service (see later section), say what services you will be selling.

Marketing and selling products

Marketing and selling a product is made easier because it is tangible, i.e. it is real, people can touch it and try it. For example, selling a car is made easier because potential customers can look at it, sit in it, drive it, etc. For customers this gives them reassurance that they are making the right decision about buying the right car.

So when selling products our challenge is to get potential customers to visit us. Once they are in the showroom or shop, etc. we can help them make the right decision.

 **action**

Answer this question – what will be the three main reasons customers come into my premises to try my products?

Marketing and selling a service

Services, on the other hand, reflecting their definition, are a much riskier purchase as they are intangible. At the time of purchasing a service, unlike the car example above, we cannot look at it or touch it, etc. so we feel more concerned that we may or may not be making the right decision (and we don't like people being uncertain about buying!). And this is made worse by not owning anything after we have purchased a service. If we purchase the wrong car, we can sell it again; it will be an expensive mistake but we may get some money back. After we have purchased the wrong service, we have nothing to sell to recover some of our money so the sense of loss is greater.

So how do we market and sell our service? How do we reduce the risk for the purchaser? When buying a service the purchaser will look for some evidence of tangibility, i.e. some evidence that the service is of good quality. How do they do this? Simply, they make a judgment about the person who is selling the service to them. If they believe and therefore trust the seller, they are much more likely to buy the service. For them the 'seller' represents a physical manifestation of the intangible. Marketing a service is about having the right person to do the marketing/selling.

But we need to make the purchase of our service as low risk as possible, so what else can we do in our marketing? We are often reassured by evidence that other people have already used this service and are satisfied by it. So copies of complimentary letters from customers are helpful or even details of customers that potential buyers can talk to (especially important in business-to-business markets). Another use of customers is the so-called 'reference customer'. Say you are an HR consultant (a service) and you regularly work for a major high-profile lawyer for placing senior staff in the firm. Everyone in that industry knows that law firm is a very respectable business with very high standards, so effectively if you are good enough for them, then you must be good enough to use. You will therefore tell (within limits of confidentiality) other prospective customers of your work with this firm and they will be impressed. By giving them this reassurance you have made purchasing your service less risky for them.

Another way of marketing services and reducing the risk for customers is to develop your brand. As we will see later in this chapter, brand is about an emotional bond between your customers and you. If your brand is trustworthy, then customers will trust your services. Financial services are examples of risky purchases. Think about buying a pension; you will give money to a firm each month for 40 years on the basis that they promise to pay you a pension starting in 40 years' time. How risky is that? So we notice that financial service firms invest lots of money in building their brand, emphasising their history and their quality, trust etc. How can you use similar tactics in helping your customers to trust you?

 **action**

If you will be offering a service (or services), list and briefly explain how you will make your service tangible, e.g.:

- Who will market/sell the service?
- What makes them right for the task?
- What guarantees will you offer customers?

- What testimonials will you provide?
- Do you have or can you get reference customers?
- Etc.

Business-to-business or business-to-consumer?

There are two types of markets:

- Business-to-Business (B2B).
- Business-to-Consumer (B2C).

B2B is about selling products/services to other businesses. They buy them either to resell (e.g. a shop) or to use those goods in the production of their products (e.g. raw materials).

B2C is about selling to individuals who buy products or services for their own use.

 **action**

Which markets will you be in? Why?

It is possible to be in both, but if so we must use two approaches because marketing in B2B and marketing in B2C are different in a number of ways, shown in the following table

For the B2B markets the main approach is about building relationships. Partly because you will want to sell to the same people again, as there are fewer buyers, but also because getting decisions made in firms often requires you to have good relationships with several people, e.g. the purchasing manager, the director, etc. Selling B2B may

> for the B2B markets the main approach is about building relationships

B2B customers	B2C customers
Tend to be a smaller number.	Tend to be a very large number.
May be in geographical clusters.	May be spread across the country.
Tend to have more complex decision-making processes involving more than one person.	Buying decisions more often made by one person.
Tend to want reliability, proven ability and to avoid/reduce the risk and cost of failure.	Can be faster to try new things.
Tend to consider price more.	Tend to consider price less.
Tend to be more objective in purchasing decision.	Tend to be more emotional in purchasing decisions.
Tend to be sold to by salespeople (easier when fewer customers).	Tend to make their own selection of products/services (necessary if large numbers of customers).

also take a longer time as businesses tend to be slower to try new things. And this isn't a lack of innovation on their behalf – it is a greater appreciation of the consequences of making a wrong decision. Say you buy flour to make cakes and you change flour supplier. If the flour is different (not wrong, just different so the cakes have a different texture) it may generate more customer complaints, causing a loss of goodwill, downtime in the factory whilst the problem is sorted, etc. So it may take you more time to swap to a different flour supplier. Of course the flip side is once they do use you, if all goes well they are likely to be slow to leave you.

B2C can still be about relationships, think of your favourite pub where they know you well, but it can be more about numbers of customers. If your product is relatively low cost you need to sell lots to make money. So with the best will in the world you cannot have a long chat with every customer. You will, of course, talk with them but you need to be mindful of time and money.

Individuals are, however, often easier to sell to because we can introduce emotion and excitement. Plus, we are often only trying to approach and convince one person and that is always easier than convincing a group of people more common in B2B . Think about where you go to buy a new car. Likely an elegant show-room, lots of glass, steel and bright lights, etc. – all very seductive (and very much part of the marketing and sales process). Now, where do you go to buy a new van? A less glamorous showroom at the back of an industrial estate. Why? Because a van is a busi-ness purchase and so you are much more focused on whether it does the job, how low you can get the price down so that you'll impress the boss, etc. B2C is about making the customer feel good, helping them into a car they will feel good about driving (and making the neighbours look!).

This isn't about saying one is better than the other; you can be very successful in either and both B2B and B2C are exceptionally good markets. And you can be in both, but the discussion here is to prompt you to consider that you need different approaches to each market. For example, you may have a website for con-sumers to purchase your products and a sales team for dealing with B2B customers. Or you may split them more on customer value, e.g. for customers buying only a small amount of product per year, you provide them with a call centre number to call; for larger ordering customers you have them visited by a member of a team (but not the same person); and for the largest customers you give them a dedicated relationship manager.

 **action**

What will be your approach to your chosen market(s)?

How do you want the world to perceive your business?

What do you think about Volkswagen and its cars? Probably, at least in the UK, good cars, a bit above average in quality and upmarket, a sensible purchase, etc. Now what do you think of Seat cars (also part of Volkswagen Audi Group)? Probably youthful, sporty, modern, etc. Consider which one is more upmarket, Lexus or Toyota? Yes, Lexus. Now why do we think Volkswagen is sensible, Seat is youthful and Lexus is more upmarket than Toyota? Because the marketing people in these companies have told us this is so.

 impact

You MUST take responsibility for what the world thinks about your business; it is too important to neglect this.

How we want to be seen is a profoundly important point and must be very clear in our business plan. There is a saying that nature abhors a vacuum, i.e. as soon as a vacuum is created, air moves in to fill the vacuum. The same with information: if there is a gap in knowledge, i.e. if people ask, 'What does that business do?', if no one knows, they will give opinions to help fill this 'information vacuum'. Now, if we don't know something, we tend to guess: sometimes we guess right and sometimes wrong. And people use guesses of other people and … this all becomes terribly unreliable. And suddenly of your low-price business people are saying, 'I've heard they are expensive'. Now throw into this mix of misinformation your competitors (who have a vested interest in not presenting you in the best light), and your reputation is in tatters.

So we must ensure that we have a clear set of messages that will resonate with our chosen market, and that we consistently and repetitively present them. Being consistent is important in all aspects of our business. So we use our:

- Mission statement.
- Marketing materials.
- Prices.
- People.
- Premises.
- Etc.

Recently in our village I saw the van of a tradesperson; a large van, dark green (not white), with elegant signwriting on the side. Now the default tradesperson's van is white as white vans are the cheapest and there are more second-hand ones available. But a media image has built up of 'white van man' and it isn't a wholly positive one. So this smart, dark green van stands out as being a bit higher quality. Even before we have spoken to anyone, we have a higher impression of this business. I'm unsure if this was the impression desired by the firm, but they have started well. We have to work to a budget and sometimes we have to accept less than perfection, but we must always seek to give a good impression. And on a new, large van, metallic paint is an extra £400 or so; not much extra for a very different impression?

 **action**

List the three main ways you want your business to be perceived.

How will you communicate these messages?

What's in a name … ?

'What's in a name? That which we call a rose
By any other name would smell as sweet.'

Romeo and Juliet (II, ii, 43) William Shakespeare

A business has to have a name, otherwise how will anyone know about it, find it or refer to it? Therefore you must name your business. The odd thing about naming a business is it could be everything or it could be nothing. Why nothing? Well, there are some fine examples where the name appears to have no connection to company, product or customer: Apple – the computer company, Lotus – a sports car company (also a software company) … and when was the last time you bought a car phone from the Carphone Warehouse?

So is it worth thinking about a name when apparently any name will do? The answer is yes, because what the examples above have is that their 'brand' has now surpassed their name. In other words, how customers feel about the brand of Apple is more important than what they feel about the word 'apple'.

And what customers feel is the first important point here. The name for your business has to resonate with your chosen target customer groups. It has to appeal to them and has to fit with them. And, here is a link to Chapter 3, it should fit with what your business is about. A good example is the fashion retailer Next, that very clearly is about new fashion once or twice a year so it has sales that empty the whole store for the next season's fashion lines. It is about the 'next' fashion for its chosen customers of mainly younger people stretching towards the middle-aged who read lots of magazines and are interested in the 'next' trend.

Related to this is how customers *feel* about the name and, linking to this chapter, is how the business wants to be placed in the marketplace, e.g. down-market, higher end, etc., and for that positioning of the firm.

> what customers feel is the first important point

Some factors to consider in the marketplace are listed in the table below.

Are your customers young or old?	Younger people often prefer to have funkier, shorter names, older people often prefer more established-sounding names.
Is your business international?	Will your name work in different markets/languages?
Do you sell fun, short-life products or very serious things?	Very serious things like legal services need a very serious name.
Is it a person business?	Does your business name need to give personality?
Is it you alone or will there be several people?	Your name as the business name or a new identity?

Some examples (all intended to be fictional, so apologies if any are real!) of types of business names are:

- Does what it says on the tin, e.g. 'Tidy Gardens'.
- A traditional name, e.g. 'Smith & Williams Solicitors'.
- An abstract name, e.g. 'Haddock' (for a design business).
- A personal service, e.g. 'Claire's Decorators'.
- A global business, e.g. 'Global Exhaust Solutions'.
- An aspirational name, e.g. 'A Better You'.

Another factor to consider is that names will be shortened – indeed you may want them to be. It seems almost too difficult to understand but the easier and quicker the name is to say, the more readily people say it, the more they will say it. People in offices, builders and young people always seem to be shortening things. Whether it is text messaging (texting) or whether people are increasingly time-poor ... who knows? But the trend is there, especially amongst younger people. For example:

● Is it Mercedes Benz or is it Mercedes?

● Do people talk about Jaguar or Jag?

● Is it a BMW (a lot of syllables) or is it a 'Beemer'?

So how customers feel about your name and in a possibly shortened form is important. An additional point here is that with some marketing skill and of course some good fortune, your name could become the byword for all products of its type, e.g. Biro (for ballpoint pens), FedEx (for couriers), Tipp-Ex (for correction fluid). Your name may even become a new verb, e.g. Google (for 'to search').

The second point about your business name, and nowadays equally important, whether you can get the domain name for your website. It is essential for all businesses to have a website so you will need the domain name, and for most businesses it will be similar to your business name. We now have almost the reverse situation to what has happened in the past, in that you may choose your business name from a list of names for which you could get the domain name. In other words, if your business is Williams Pigs, can you get a relevant domain name, e.g. www. WilliamsPigs.co.uk?

In summary, your business name must be chosen on a balance of:

● Your chosen market and your chosen customers.

● A reflection of how you want to position your business relevant to your competitors.

● Whether you can buy the relevant domain name.

How you decide your business name is up to you, but the process should be as follows:

- Gather a few people together (your business partner(s), friends, family, etc.).
- Explain what your business will be about, how it will be positioned, who the customers will be, etc.
- Write some choices on a piece of paper.
- Check on-line if you can get the domain names.
- From the possible names for which you can buy the domain name(s) pick a name, perhaps by voting or, as its your business, you choose!).

Remember, your business name is a reflection of your business and not you yourself, but you need to finally choose a name you like and feel proud of saying.

 **action**

- Write the name of your business.
- Give a one sentence reason for choosing it.
- Give the domain name(s) you have bought/registered.

Which customers don't you want?

'All of them' I hear many people say? Ah ... no. All customers are not created equal. From some you will never make any money; they will take a lot of time and then place small orders, they will complain most, they will be the slowest to pay their invoices, and they will just be difficult.

 **timesaver**

If you refuse to work with the difficult customers, you have a double winner: not only are they not wasting your time, they are now customers of your competitors and wasting their time!

You pick your customers and not the other way around. And the reason for this is that by being selective you will have a better relationship with your customers. Say you make bread and you set about telling the world. You are going to spend a fortune in trying to get the message to as many people as possible. And you will spend some of that money telling people who don't buy bread (waste of money there). And then of those who do receive your marketing communications, some of them will not buy your bread because you have made white and they want brown. And then some like sliced and some like unsliced. And some like organic. And for some it is too expensive and for others it is too cheap, and some like ... it goes on. It is a little like shouting into the wind and hoping someone will hear.

Better to be selective and choose a target group. Because once we have we can then make products/services that are really good for them. Instead of trying to make a single product to please the world (cannot be done) we make a product that we know pleases our chosen customer group. And because we have a well-defined customer group or 'segment', we can communicate with them better as we know which newspapers they read, where they shop, how they like our website to look/work, etc. It seems counterintuitive and it does take bravery, as we are saying which customers we *don't* want, but by focusing on a segment we can make products/services that really work for our chosen customers.

better to be selective and choose a target group

 **action**

Describe your target customers in as much detail as possible.

And how do we know what our customers really want? Because we ask them. As mentioned earlier we want to be discreet about our plans to prevent our competitors finding out what we are doing. But there will come a time when we have to ask some target customers what they like/want. Of course there is some risk here, so we do it carefully, i.e. don't tell them everything but say you are looking into people buying X and wonder what they like about their existing product/supplier/offer, etc. The key point is this is real market research, as asking friends and family will only get you so far and they may be unduly kind to you!

 **action**

Do market research by asking target customers about their existing product/supplier/offer. Present your findings, to help demonstrate there is a need for your products/services/company.

The frustration about doing market research is that it tells you what people 'say' they will buy. And not that they definitely will put their hands in their pockets and buy what you are offering; you won't know until you have started trading. So is market research worth doing? Well, it has got to be better than no market research.

Is the market big enough?

So here are customers we don't want and market research that may show only limited demand for what we are planning to offer. Great! And exactly why am I reading this book to prove my business idea has no merit? Well, we said at the start the Business Plan isn't by itself wholly useful, but it is the process we go through and the questions we answer that helps us build a better business. And even if there is no demand here, then we can look elsewhere.

What we must do is:

(a) demonstrate that there is a market,
(b) estimate how large a market there is, and
(c) seek to determine if it is growing.

And before you say what I think you are about to say, yes, it is nearly impossible to do reliably, but we can and have to make some calculations to prove, if nothing else, that we are not wasting our time.

So how do we do it? A number of ways are possible and we may need to gather data in more than one of these ways and combine them to give some estimation of the size of the market. For example:

- If you are going into a big market/industry, then it is likely a market research firm will have studied the market/industry and published a market review report. Perfect, job done. Ah, maybe, as these reports are usually not cheap, perhaps £5,000. Worthwhile if you are planning a reasonably sized new business, so you can justify the money. Or if you are lucky, you might be able to borrow one from a library.

- The business newspapers have articles about industries that may have data useful to you.

- Use internet material.

- You can ask your prospective customers – if you go to the biggest retailer and they sell 50,000 units a year, then from that you could extrapolate what the others do and get the total market.

- You could find a business mentor, who has experience in the market you are planning to enter.

- You could pay a market research/consultancy firm to do the market research for you.

- You could calculate from the beginning, e.g. we are about to have the outside woodwork of our house painted (and the sealed units replaced, as mentioned before). So if you were planning a painting and decorating business in our village your estimate would look like this:

  - Approximately 5,000 people.

  - That means approximately 1,700 houses/bungalows.

  - If this job needs to be done every five years that is about 340 houses to have the outside painted per year.

  - Say 30% have uPVC double glazing (so no need to paint) – the 30% is an estimation, but it is likely this figure can be found on the internet – so that is about 200 houses per year that need painting.

  - If the market price is about £900, then the annual market value of painting the 200 houses per year in the village is £180,000 per year.

  - How many painters and decorators are there in the village? Say three, so each could earn £60,000 p.a. (sounds like a feasible living). If ten decorators, then only £18,000 each, if all get an equal share, and that doesn't sound so attractive.

  - It is also worth calculating it from a time perspective to see if the figure is similar. If painting each house takes four or five days, then a painter and decorator is likely to earn for 45 weeks (52 weeks minus some holiday minus three weeks for bad weather – but could do inside painting then?), so 45 weeks at £900 equals about £40,500. Attractive?

● Also try to find out if this market is growing, staying the
  same, or declining. Ask some perspective customers if they
  are painting their house more or less often. And you could,
  again slightly sneaky here, ask someone who lives in the
  village to call the existing decorators to say they are thinking
  about having their house painted and how quickly can they
  can start? Immediate starts mean they have little work. All
  booked up for three months and you may have spotted a
  market here.

 **action**

Present the results of your research and calculations to describe the size of
your chosen market. Show, with information, if it is growing, staying the
same, or declining.

Setting prices

'Price is what you pay. Value is what you get.'

> Warren Buffett – a leading investor

A number of methods for setting our prices exist. Some obvious
and some less so, but it is important we give thought to setting
the right prices. Some important considerations about price:

● You choose the price.

● Price is the only part of the marketing mix that generates
  income (all other factors are costs).

● Your prices say something about you business – so it has to
  be consistent with your other marketing messages.

● Price and cost are different.

● Reducing prices is easy and raising prices is difficult –
  always start high.

Ideally we do not want our customers to consider the price in making a decision; we want them to buy the product/service because it is right. In reality (but surprisingly not always) the price does enter the sales conversation. But people use price to make an opinion not only about the product/service but also about you and your business, so it is important to get the price right from the start.

> ideally we do not want our customers to consider the price in making a decision

Methods to set prices include:

- Internal methods:
  - Cost+ pricing.
  - Margins pricing.
  - Time-based pricing.
- External methods:
  - Market range.
  - Competitor pricing and market positioning pricing.
  - Dynamic pricing.
- Value-based pricing:

The most common way to set a price for most people new to a business is some sort of 'cost+' model. In this way we work out what a product costs to produce and then add something extra (mark-up). For example:

- Cost of making the product = £47.
- Mark-up of 10% = £4.70.
- Price to the customer = £51.70.

Relatively easy to do when we know all our costs. Not so easy in the first phase of our business (as we may not know all our costs), plus this works by knowing how much we will sell, again not so easy in the early days. It is also more difficult when we have multiple products (say some simple and some more complex to produce) and how do we apportion the fixed costs like the office rent? Nonetheless, it is a reasonable place to start and it does help us to address the issue of price needing to be above cost.

Margin pricing is the other side of the same coin. Instead of setting a 10% profit on the cost price you decide to make 10% profit of the sale price, e.g. price of £50, a margin is 10%, is £5.

Time-based pricing is very common amongst professionals such as lawyers, consultants, etc. For example, you charge a fee per day for your time whilst working for a client. Say you charge £600 per day: you will either charge per unit of time (one local law firm asks its staff to record time on a 0.1 hour basis) or you will charge a fixed price for the job (project) based upon your estimation of the time it will take you times your daily rate. Your 'daily rate' tends to be a preoccupation amongst consultants, especially the self-employed, with some not wanting to say what their rate is but wanting to know others' – a good gossip! There is a whole bunch of factors that affect your daily rate, e.g. sector, the speciality of your knowledge, the length of the project, etc., but my experience is that much less than £200 per day isn't enough to run a business on (e.g. three days a week gives £30k); £300–£600 is typical, £800 is a good rate and outside of special sectors (like finance), consistently achieving more than £1,000 a day is not so common. In areas like city deals and with specialist lawyers, tax advisors, etc. then £3,000–5,000 per day is achievable if you have a big-name brand behind you.

The above are all valuable pricing strategies and many people start there. The big issue is that whilst ultimately we choose the price we want (or we walk away), it is the customers who finally decide so our pricing method has to be based on the marketplace. In reality we often use a combination of the internal and the market-based (external) approach.

When you last bought a tyre for your car (or ask someone who has), what price did you pay? Now ask a few more people. Chances are that the results of your research will start to form a market range that has something like £30 at the lower end with quite a few people (perhaps the majority) in the £30–70 range, with some up to £100, a few between £100 to £200 and only a small percentage above £200 who have specialist vehicles, e.g. 4×4 or very high performance. So if you are setting up a business to sell tyres you now have a range to aim at. If you want to sell tyres at £500 then you must have very good reasons for doing so and be able to prove (real hard evidence) to potential customers that those tyres are worth the money (and the percentage of the customers that will pay this much will be small).

 **action**

What is the price range present in your chosen market?

Now we have the market range we can factor in the effect of competitors; this is an approach that is about **competitor pricing and market positioning**. In many markets, not in all and not in all cultures but enough to consider, this underlying piece of psychology: if your product/service is better than competitor A, your customers will expect it to have a higher price than competitor A. It is one of the ways that customers decide, amongst you and your competitors, who is better than whom. The reverse also applies: i.e. if we are worse (we don't usually say worse, we say better value), our customers expect a lower price than competitor A.

So in setting our product/service price we look at the competitors we are choosing to compete with and price according to who we are better than and who better value than. We have to remember that price is a very visible signal to customers about who we are, so pricing has to be consistent with the position in the market and has to be consistent with our marketing strategy and our mission/values.

Consider the BMW 3 Series and the Mercedes-Benz C-Class; they are similarly priced. And both priced more than the equivalent Ford Mondeo as they consider themselves to be more up-market than the Ford and price is one of the signals to the market that this is so. (Most of the cars in these ranges are built in Western Europe so the cost of production doesn't wholly explain the price differences.)

A final thought on market-based pricing is that of **dynamic pricing**. This reflects the availability or lack of availability of your product in the market. This could be a reflection of the underlying product, e.g. a stock or share, or the price of oil, or the price of fish at the daily market. Or it could reflect the current supply situation, e.g. in short supply or in excess supply. If something is in short supply the price goes up; when there is excess, the price goes down. For example, recent increases in the price of petrol and car taxation policies have led to a big demand for small, used cars even to the extent that used car prices have been increasing (usually they go down, often dramatically). In some markets, customers expect and are used to the price changing, but in other markets it appears to cause confusion. So some businesses go for dynamic pricing (e.g. domestic central heating oil) whilst others accept the risk by having a higher, more stable price and when the market price goes down, they make more profit (and perhaps have some time making a temporary loss).

Another aspect of dynamic pricing is a reflection of product availability on a geographical basis. Supermarkets tend to use dynamic pricing to reflect location, e.g. your milk from the local 'convenience' branch of the supermarket may be more expensive than at a larger branch of the same chain. The convenience factor is something customers will reward the retailer with a price premium.

Also consider the dynamic pricing of products across our product/service range, e.g. do we have the same profit on all products/services? No. If the customer will buy one thing and then move up the range, we can price lower for the first entry level product/service and then have progressively higher profits up the range, cars, for example. Or we can sell the product cheaply and then have a much higher profit on consumable items, e.g. inkjet printers, where the printer is cheap and the ink cartridges expensive.

We can see that a combination of internal and external factors drive the prices we charge. But there is another way and that is **value-based** pricing. So instead of pricing according to the cost of providing the product/service (internal) or relative to the market rate (external), we charge what the product or service is worth to the customer. If, driving along the motorway, you develop a bad headache, you will turn off at the Services to buy some painkillers. How much will you pay for those painkillers? 50p, £1, £2, more? Indeed, will you care how much they cost as long as they get rid of the pain? So those tablets suddenly become worth what? If our customers are suffering pain, how much will they reward us with if we provide a painkiller? Frequently a great deal. Consider another scene: the manager of a factory employing ten staff and a key machine in the production line is broken. The in-house electrician cannot fix it. And the whole factory is now idle, costing a great deal in wasted wages, failed orders, customer reputation, etc. Imagine you are an electronics engineer who can fix that machine. How much will that manager pay you to fix the machine? A great deal …

In reality people only buy things for two reasons (the same two reasons for all human motivation):

- To get away from pain.
- To go towards pleasure.

Other examples include:

- Paying an accountant to sort out a nasty tax problem – getting away from pain.
- Buying flowers for a loved one, think of the happiness that gives – towards pleasure.
- Buying new clothes that make you fell like a million dollars – towards pleasure

It is clear that value pricing has a lot going for it. It taps into the needs/wants of the customer and seeks from the customer a reward for solving their pain or giving them pleasure. It is also frequently more profitable. Consider that packet of painkillers: a packet of paracetamol will cost about 10p, so a cost+ model may lead us to price this packet at 11p or 12p or, as a retailer, we may want cost+ 200% to 300% so we may sell it for 20p to 30p. Or value pricing may lead to 50p to £1.00. A big difference in profit!

> it is clear that value pricing has a lot going for it

 **action**

Decide on your pricing strategy.

Before deciding/considering our pricing strategy we should think about some other influences on prices:

- Your industry – drilling a hole in a piece of metal will have higher price in the oil industry then in the agriculture industry (same hole in same metal) as the former has higher expectations of cost (but will demand better service).

- Your location – people will pay more for a cake from an independent baker in a wealthier location than a poorer location.

- Your brand – people will pay more for the same item with a brand than without a brand.

There are even some rules of thumb to help us:

- In restaurants, the price of the finished dish is typically 4× the cost of the ingredients, i.e. a piece of fish bought for £5 will be on the menu at £20.

- A retailer will usually need to double the cost, i.e. product bought for £1.50 is sold for £3.00.

- A bottle of wine in a restaurant will usually be 3× the cost.

- Professionals typically work on five fee-earning hours per working day of eight hours.

As your business trades successfully you will be able to calculate your own rules of thumb.

 **brilliant** timesaver

It is easy to reduce prices but very difficult, sometimes impossible, to increase prices. Never start too low – you will never get them up again.

Other factors/tactics to consider in pricing:

Do you want to skim or penetrate?

Skimming is where we set a high price to take or skim off the top end of the market. This way we take the highest price and potentially the greatest profit. A commonly used strategy with new technology (and with differentiation or focus strategies) as this higher profit margin can be used to pay back the R&D cost of the products/service. Then we can keep the price high (think

Dyson vacuum cleaners) or reduce it over time (think smartphone) as the product gets older and other, better, products emerge in the market.

Penetration is when we seek to get market share, i.e. we launch the product and want to sell lots quickly. Reasons for this include to outwit competitors, build a presence, allow our factory to operate on bigger volumes so making production cheaper, etc. Frequently we launch with a regular price reduced for a limited time.

Pricing is obviously important to get right. So before launching we do need to test it with a number of people from our chosen market. We obviously want to do this discreetly to avoid alerting our competitors but it is worth taking the risk. So we don't want to do it publicly but want to do it by talking in person to target customers. Best to do it as late as possible as, even if competitors hear about it, they may not have so much time to act. Once we are in business, some of our new products/services will be designed for existing customers with whom we have relationships and therefore these discussions will be easier.

brilliant questions and answers

Q If the price in the market isn't making you any money – are you in the right market?

A If yes, you have to work differently to enable the market price to go up or your costs to go down.

A If no, then move your business into another market.

There will be some markets we simply cannot make money in, so we should move on. Or, and this works sometimes, take the market price and work backwards to design a product/service that fits the price. A few years ago I visited a fish processing factory. On the production lines they had a 'cod fish pie' and a 'fish pie'. The second was because the retailer wanted to sell the product flash labelled at 99p and at that price, cod was too expensive so they used other, cheaper forms of white fish.

 **tip**

We have to price to help make others in the retail chain make money – else why would they stock our products?

A final key point about pricing is further down the line in our product reaching the customers. If we make something that we sell to another person for them to sell, i.e. as is typical in supplying retailers, then we have to consider their need to make money. So a typical scenario is:

Cost of our making something	£7	e.g. to cover raw materials, time.
We sell it to the retailer at	£14	e.g. to cover our overheads, profit.
They sell (retail) it at	£30	e.g. to cover their costs, profit.

And the more the number of people between you and the final customer, the more everyone needs to make a profit and the more the price goes up. I recall one person who had designed a clever new product that they wanted to sell direct to shops, but in that industry they encountered resistance from the shops that didn't want to buy direct (even thought they would make more!); they would only buy through their existing wholesale distribution chain. So they sold to a wholesale who sold to another wholesaler who sold to … and in the worst situation they were selling for £10, but the product was nearly £150 in the final shop. That caused them problems as customers had £150 quality expectations for a £10 product. Perhaps an extreme example, but we do need to factor in everyone's costs and profits in setting prices for us and them.

brilliant tip

We make our money when we buy and not when we sell – if we pay too much when buying anything our chance of making profits is reduced or removed.

To discount or not to discount?

brilliant tip

Rule #1 – you never give unless they give in return.

Discounting is a form of negotiation and is Rule #1 in negotiation.

brilliant example

Imagine the scene of a salesperson (and this mistake is made by inexperienced salespeople) with a prospective customer, selling office paper for the printers, photocopies, etc. Sitting in the purchasing manager's office the salesperson senses a deal is imminent and quite correctly asks the manager if they want to go ahead.

Purchasing manager   'I like the offer and your product but the price is a little too high.'

Salesperson   'Ok, I'll give you 5% discount.'

What will the Purchasing manager say next?

Purchasing manager   'Thank you, but it is still a little expensive.'

Why? Well, the salesperson gave something away without requiring anything in return. In effect they rewarded the purchasing manager for asking for a discount. So naturally the purchasing manager will ask again, and will keep doing so if continually rewarded. What the salesperson should have said is:

Salesperson   'If you agree to sign the purchase order today I can give
               you a 5% discount' or
               'If you double your order I can find you a discount of 20%.'

Or … whatever is right in the situation … but the key point is the salesperson only ever 'gives' if the customer gives in return.

A discount policy is fine but it has to be a considered policy that makes sense for your business. A discount policy is ok because it allows us to keep the original price in the market and we remember that that price is helping the customers to judge our quality/positioning. But a discount policy allows us to reward certain customers who give us benefits. Reasons for giving a discount include:

> a discount policy is fine but it has to be a considered policy that makes sense for your business

- Customer is buying in higher volumes – increases income, increases production volumes, means the customer may not be using our competitors.
- Customer is buying regularly (helps to keep your production efficient and low cost).
- Customer agrees to sign a longer-term purchasing contract.
- Customer agrees to pay (fully or partially) at the time of order.
- Customer agrees to take deliveries at our choice or times (so we can fit their order into production to suit us).

 **action**

Will you discount? If so, what will be your discount policy?

Give your prices for your initial products and services. Show your profit margins at these prices.

Build a brand (and avoid competition?)

'Brand' is, like 'no-frills', a business term that has entered everyday language. We talk about buying branded products or non-branded products. Yet everything is made by someone so isn't everything a brand?

Well, there are groups of definitions of 'brand' that refer to the name, logos, etc. that identify a brand. And the origin of branded goods is that 'branding' was using a hot iron to mark (or brand) packing cases with the company name to confer authenticity of the goods. In those days there was a temptation amongst the unscrupulous to fake the goods, i.e. pass them off as the genuine article (of course this still happens!). Putting their company name to a product was a way of the reputable business saying 'this is a genuine product'.

Brands, however, are now about how customers (and others) feel about the company. There is an intention to create an emotional connection with the brand (and thereby the company). Brand is about a story and creating and telling that story.

And that is how we distinguish branded and non-branded goods; with a branded product or service we feel an emotional attachment to the brand. It makes us feel different and in some way better, be it excited, reassured, more successful, etc. Think about how you feel about your favourite brand of clothing. What words do you use to describe that brand? Are they emotional words?

Perhaps this is sounding all rather touchy-feely for some readers. Why are we talking about it now? Because brands are powerful. Do these words indicate trust in and how you feel good about the brand and its products and services? So you are likely to buy from the company again? Good. And you don't really think about the price? Good.

Brand therefore becomes an exceptionally powerful source of competitive advantage. And remember, our whole business is about achieving a source of competitive advantage.

But even more useful for us is that brand can become a source of 'sustainable' competitive advantage. We previously considered products and services and we should consider their sustainability:

- Products can be copied – if we launch a successful product our rivals can buy one, take it apart, find out how it works, and then if they choose to they can copy it and can make and sell their own version of it. And because they didn't have to spend money developing it, they can probably make it at lower cost and make more money. And unless we have taken steps to protect our intellectual property, chances are they may get away with it! So our source of sustainability may be compromised.

- Services are more difficult to copy as the customer's perception of quality is very much linked to the quality of the person delivering the service. And this isn't so easy to copy. Consider your local major fast food restaurant. These types of firm tend to spend a great deal in training their staff and whilst they rarely give poor service there is a difference between different staff and some are just better than others. Not impossible to copy this level of good service but it takes time and money (if it were easy, good service would be everywhere!). Now consider the service and relationship a partner in a law firm has with their clients; could we put a new person in post and expect the same level of service? Very unlikely. Service, compared to product, is therefore difficult to copy thus giving us a stronger source of competitive advantage.

- Brands are very difficult to copy. Think about two brands you like in an industry, say the car industry or the fashion industry. How do you feel about those brands? Chances are you feel different things about them and that is to be expected. Do you think another brand could displace what you feel about them? Probably not. Once a brand occupies a place in our heart and mind it is very difficult to copy it or to displace it. A brand therefore gives us a competitive advantage and one that is very difficult (almost impossible?) to copy. A *sustainable* competitive advantage.

 **action**

How will you use branding to help you achieve a greater sustainability in your business?

For some sectors it is essential to create a brand. For example the fashion industry is very brand-driven. A pair of jeans is just a pair of jeans until they have a brand attached. Now for some customers, all that matters is low price and they don't want to pay for a brand, so in cost leadership brand may not be afford-able. But for many other customers the brand of clothing is very important and something we need to develop. And in many other industries brand is associated with our reputation, so it is important in service industries. It is something we must attend to if we are to build sustainability.

 **timesaver**

Like price, it is easy to take a brand downmarket but very difficult to take it upmarket. Consider this if you are planning a brand and never start too low – unless you mean to stay low.

Internet marketing

Whatever business you are starting you must have a website. Obviously if we are beginning an internet business this will be the case anyway. And if we are planning a big business, it is likely we will be planning a website. But it continues to amaze me how many small businesses do not have a website. And they are making a big mistake. Not because they are not selling via the internet but because they are invisible.

If you are under 45 years of age, ask yourself when you last looked in a telephone directory for a number. If you are over 45, ask someone younger. Ask someone in their teens and chances are they may not even answer. If we want to find a number now we will call a directory enquiry service or we will look on the internet. I've been looking for a car and it is remarkable how some garages cannot be found on the web. Yet I talk to many bigger garages and they have people from all over the country coming to buy cars from them. It gives them a much larger market. And for what cost? Maybe only £300?

The fact is that a very large proportion of people looking to buy something begin their search by looking on the internet. If you are not there you are not on their list of potential suppliers. And the younger your chosen customer group the more likely they are to *only* look on the internet. Think about the growth of smart phones (like the Apple iPhone) which give internet access to people on the move – those potential customers do not even need a computer to look for a supplier.

Websites come in many shapes and forms (and costs); below is a list moving from the simplest to the most complex.

- Electronic business card.
- The web-based version of your brochure.
- The order placing system (with off-line manual processing of your order).
- The order receiving system with automated processing of order.
- The full e-commerce website with integrated database.

A basic 'electronic business card' website will be single page (or perhaps up to five pages) that will say who you are, what your business does and give your contact details. This is your first step in being on the internet and crucially it makes your business visible. Today I have just ordered some new double-glazed sealed units from a company with just such a website. First I used Google to search for 'sealed units' + Norwich, where I found a company listed on a directory website that had a map showing the location of the firm, clicked on its flag on the map, and clicked on their website, which is a three-page website of 'Home', 'Products and Services' and 'Contact us'. Called the number, spoke with a very helpful (and therefore convincing) lady (I've never before bought sealed units) and placed the order. There is no other way I would have found that business. How much for such a website? Broadly you will pay:

- £10 to register your domain name (per annum to renew).
- £250 for someone to design and produce your website. There are lots of good freelancers at this price. A company will charge more and a student likely less.
- £150 for a reliable company to host your website. You don't want to leave your PC on all the time so best pay to have it hosted.

So, in total, £400 to have your very important presence on the web for your first year.

Once there the next option is to put your products and service catalogue on your website. In effect your website becoming your shop window. In fact, for many businesses, is there a need to print a catalogue? They are expensive to produce, are immediately out of date and heavy to post. How much easier (and cheaper) to email your customers with a link to your new online catalogue. Critically, it is easy to change prices to reflect demand (up and down). Of course for some markets a paper catalogue is still the right thing to do but the internet gives us options. For those markets the website is still likely to be in the hundreds of pounds plus the photography of the products (but you have to do that for the catalogue anyway).

Thereafter it is a move to being an internet business, with your website now effectively a working shop with customers placing their orders online. At the simplest level the orders arrive electronically and one of the staff manually processes the payment details. Next is a system where the customer's credit card is processed in real time. Finally we have an e-commerce website supported by a database. Think eBay where the system automatically emails to tell you sellers you have bought from previously have listed other products; think Amazon with its customised home page when you log on, etc. For sites like these expenditure can be a few thousand pounds to database-driven sites for hundreds of thousands of pounds. It may sound like a lot of money but think how many customers can buy 24 hours a day, with very little staff intervention (with the attendant cost savings).

 **action**

What sort of website will you have? Give reasons for your choice. Allocate some costs in your budget.

 recap

- Marketing will make or break your business – harness its power.

- Who will your customers be? When we have a clear picture of who our customers are, we can tailor our offering and our business to particularly resonate with this group or groups.

- Price and cost are different and not connected. Pricing strategy needs careful consideration and, if possible, value pricing is the most attractive.

- Remember, you have to be on the internet. Even if you are not an internet-based business. If you have no website you are invisible to a large number of customers.

- Brands may be the solution to reducing competition.

CHAPTER 5

Making money

The most popular part of
the plan!

'My other piece of advice, Copperfield,' said Mr Micawber, 'you know "Annual income twenty pounds, annual expenditure nineteen nineteen six, result happiness. Annual income twenty pounds, annual expenditure twenty pounds nought and six, result misery."'

Charles Dickens, *David Copperfield*

I recall a story (that I hope is true) about Prof. Stephen Hawking and his exceptionally successful book *A Brief History of Time*. In dealing with the big things of the universe it was inevitable there would be many scientific concepts and equations necessary to explain it all. But the publisher told Prof. Hawking that for every equation he put into the book, he would halve sales. Prof. Hawking took this on board and in the end included only one equation $E = mc^2$ (as he felt this too important to leave out). I mention this here as I fear the more I talk about the accounts side of business, the more readers will turn away. Not good for this book but more important than that, many people who would benefit and enjoy running their own business may inadvertently allow the accounts part to turn them away from what is a very good thing to do. Don't let this happen, keep with it and the numbers will all make sense!

 **tip**

Money is like blood; it only does any good if it circulates.

Whilst we might admire someone for being clever, funny, exciting, beautiful, successful, we rarely admire them for their circulatory system. But beneath every clever, funny, exciting, beautiful successful person is a circulatory system. Beneath every successful business is a money system.

And if I'm honest, the money and the accounts side bores me rigid as well, but I have enough experience to know it is very important. So let's keep it simple and focus on the important parts. (Accountants love this side of things and they can deal with the rest of it ... and you'll know enough to keep an eye on them!)

Money talks ...

The bottom line is that your business has to make money. If you are not comfortable with this fact then perhaps you have reached the end of the line with this Business Plan (and this book). I hope you have enjoyed the journey, that you have found things interesting and maybe learnt something along the way. Farewell and I wish you all the very best for the future.

However, if you *are* comfortable with this fact ... I hope you are ... thank you, and we should continue ...

It is surprising how often someone says they have a great idea and when you ask them how it will make money they look confused ... and mutter something about 'it will in time'. You have no time. Most businesses die in the first year because they run out of money.

And it is easy to understand why we sometimes fall into this trap. Slightly confusingly, we have a number of internet businesses (particularly at this time of social media websites) that may not currently make money, have no obvious way of making money, and may not make money for many years. Yet they appear to be worth hundreds of millions of pounds, e.g. Twitter and Facebook. This is a different world and is a special part of new business start-ups. The thing here is that the founders are not usually using their own money. They are using other people's money and it is usually less painless to lose other people's money than your own! More about this in Chapter 6.

And we should clarify a final point: there is no such thing as a not-for-profit (or non-profit) organisation. We might be running a business or a social enterprise or a charity but they all have one thing in common: Mr Micawber (above) was right. The language might change, e.g. business calls it profit, public sector or charity calls it 'surplus', but it is the same thing – more money coming in than going out. Strangely enough, running the finances of a business in this respect is no different to running our own personal or household finances.

> running the finances of a business is no different to running our own personal or household finances

As mentioned at the beginning of this book, making money is not the primary reason for starting a business. But *not* making money will sure as hell be the end of the business.

How do we make money?

In business writing this is sometimes called the 'Business Model' but at its heart is the question: how does our business make its money? Implicit in this is how do we deliver value to our customers? For, looking back to Chapter 3, if we give them something of value, they will give us something of value and that is usually money.

There is one obvious way and some other, perhaps less obvious, ways of making money.

● The simplest form is a direct exchange of goods and money. We make something and sell it to someone. For example we make cupcakes that with ingredients, staff time, kitchen facilities, shop to sell them in, etc. comes to 50p for each cup cake. You sell them to other people at £2 each. We make £1.50 per cupcake sold.

Other ways of making money include:

● Selling advertising. This is the main revenue of a newspaper. It makes money by gathering together a group of people (called readers), usually a particular type of person, and then offers to companies who want to sell to that same group of people the chance to advertise in the newspaper. So those who appear to be the customers, i.e. the newspaper purchasers/readers, are not the main customers who are the advertisers. (The price we pay for a newspaper is a small part of the proprietor's income.) This model is also followed by many internet websites. The users (readers) do not pay, but the advertisers pay to have their adverts flashed in front of the users.

● Sell the finance to pay for the product/service. Used for many years in the car industry where the manufacturer and the dealer make more money selling us a loan to buy a car than they make on building and selling the car.

● Sell flexibility. Where there is a fixed price for a fixed job, but changes to the job required by the customer are charged extra and at a much higher rate. Sometimes used in construction of public projects, like roads, etc.

● Sell other add-ons, e.g. selling things like warranties when we buy electrical goods.

● Use customers' money to invest. Banks make money out of taking the money we deposit with them and lending it with interest to other people. Or some traders make money by receiving cash with the order and then paying their supplier some months later. During that time they have invested the money and made some profit.

- Doing something on behalf of your customer. It is possible to pay someone a fee to submit our tax returns to the government. So we receive little directly other than it means we will not be in trouble with the government.

- A commission basis to making money. An auction house will take your goods and sell them in the market and in return will take a percentage of the price achieved at the auction.

- Selling time. Often employed by professional services, e.g. they sell their time by the hour or by the day.

- Commission on results, e.g. a management consultant will not be paid any fee for their work but will receive a share of the costs' cut or income increased. Often heralded as a new model of working but commercial fisherman have been paid like this for over a century.

- Licensing. Customers don't buy and own the product/service, they instead pay a fee for the right to use the product/service. A lot of software is sold like this and a good example is internet security/anti-virus software where we pay an annual fee for the right to use (not own) the software.

- Freemium. Give away the basic product/service and charge for the extras, e.g. Skype, where the basic service is free but premium services attract a fee. (Once people have bought they are more likely to upgrade.)

You must be clear about how your business will make money. Which way you make it is your choice. And it will depend partly on your industry, partly on your objectives for the business and partly on how your business is financed. If you have money available you can play a longer game. If you have very little money you need to generate income quickly.

 **action**

Write a statement, no numbers, about how your business will make money. Make it short, make it clear, as nothing interests people more than a precise answer to the question, 'How will this business make money?'

Gobbledegook? Not really

> like any other specialism it has its own language and once we understand the language we can understand the money side of our business

Finance and accounts are easier to understand than you may think. Like any other specialism it has its own language and once we understand the language we can understand the money side of our business. Some key definitions are given below.

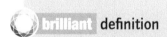 **definition**

Income
The money we receive from customers for the products/services we sell. It can also include income from bank interest, perhaps one-off sales (e.g. we sell an old van), etc

Costs (or expenditure)
The money we pay out in running our business, e.g. for supplies, utility bills, marketing costs, staff wages, etc.

Profit
The money left over when our income is larger than our costs.

Loss

The money we don't have when our costs are larger than our income.

Profit and Loss account

An annual (usually) summary of all our transactions looking back over the last 12 months. It is a historical document and tells us how well we did last year. It contains both income and expenditure but unlike a cash-flow forecast it doesn't link to the time of cash in and out of the business. Whilst usually historic can also be presented as a Profit and Loss (P&L) budget for the coming 12 months.

Balance sheet

A statement of the things you own (your assets, e.g. property) and the things that you owe (your liabilities, e.g. bank loans) for your business. So it is possible to establish how valuable or otherwise the business is. Often a historical document that measures the worth of the business on that given day (usually the last day of your financial year). A balance sheet is important for lenders (and people who may want to buy your business) as with lots of assets and few liabilities it is generally a secure, and therefore attractive, operation. It is a 'snapshot' of the business on the day it was produced (the next day it could change).

Cash

Readily spendable money. Usually real money (notes, etc), cash in the bank to which you have immediate access, unused agreed bank overdraft.

Cash-flow

The movement of cash in and out of our business.

Budget

A forward-looking allocation of income and expenditure (i.e. next year we expect £X income and £Y expenditure, usually split into headings and months).

See also the examples of a budget, cash-flow forecast, profit and loss account and balance sheet on pp. 118–21.

Cash is king!

'How little you know about the age you live in if you think that honey is sweeter than cash in hand.'

Ovid, Roman poet (43BC–17AD)

The majority of businesses that fail in their first year do so because they run out of cash. Not because their idea was not good, not because they had poor staff, not because they had no customers. But because they ran out of cash. It therefore becomes obvious that our ability to both forecast and successfully manage our cash in those early months is critical.

- Cash is:
  - physical money, i.e. notes and coins.
  - Money in bank accounts that you can access readily (not longer-term deposits that require notice).
  - Unused borrowing facilities, i.e. any unused overdraft facility (instantly available).
- Cash is not:
  - Unpaid customer invoices (not usually readily accessible as customers don't always pay).
  - Stock (again take time to turn this into cash).
  - Longer-term deposits requiring notice.

When we manage a business, we become preoccupied with 'cash-flow' which is simply the movement of cash in and out of our business. Why is it so important?

Imagine you have £10,000 in your business account and your car has just died. It is impossible for you to operate without a car and in a slight panic you hand over £10,000 to your local car dealer. Later you realise you have left yourself no money in the business account but you are relieved when checking with the office that a larger client had promised to pay their latest invoice (£20k) tomorrow. Phew! The next day your operations manager calls to say your raw materials supplier has just cancelled the latest delivery to the factory as you had not paid their last invoice of £8,000. 'Damn' you mutter, before realising the £20k due in. Today! Yes! Your finance clerk checks the bank, no money, calls your client who says they cannot pay the invoice until next week at the earliest as one of their clients has let them down. You are now stuck in a full blown cash-flow crisis. You cannot make anything because you cannot pay the invoice to release raw materials. And you cannot pay any bills because you cannot make anything to sell. And then next week is the end of the month and salaries to staff need to be paid ...

Now, if you had not used all the £10,000 for the car, some money would have been left to pay the supplier even if your client was still late in paying you. Perhaps you could have spent £5k on a car (you can always buy a better one next year) or perhaps you could have used some finance so only needed to pay £500 deposit and then paid a little every month? Whatever way the car was financed isn't so relevant here, what *is* relevant is that we need money to make money. If you'd paid £500, you would have £9,500 to pay the £8k invoice, the raw materials would have arrived, the factory back to normal, etc. Happiness. So we look to avoid ever handing over our last monies, especially large amounts. Managing the flow of money in and out of the business is therefore critical. Cash-flow is king.

Cash-flow management

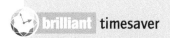 **timesaver**

Worry about cash-flow from this point forward – it will save you a lot of time and money here on in.

Being smarter at managing cash is therefore a critical skill within a new business. Tactics to improve cash-flow management include:

- Invoice the day the work is complete – there is no reason to delay ... and the invoice is less likely to be forgotten.

- Better still, invoice in stages – e.g. beginning, middle and end. No reason why you cannot agree this as part of contract negotiations.

- Even better still, invoice all upfront. Not many firms will say yes, but there is no reason not to ask, and some public sector organisations will agree if they have underspent budget at the end of the year.

- Try to avoid giving credit. It is common in B2B markets but there is no law that says you should.

- Make it someone's daily job to manage the cash-flow.

Rapidly, we come to appreciate that sitting on some cash is a very desirable position that takes out one significant worry from the business (and you). You could even then afford to pay your invoices immediately. Now some accountants may say this isn't 'efficient', but if you are sitting on some cash, what does it matter? But more importantly, a business that pays its bills immediately is a very good customer, so when you pay your suppliers' bills immediately they will value you greatly. And if they ever have a shortage of product, who do you think they will supply first?

> a business that pays its bills immediately is a very good customer

 **action**

Put a 12-month cash-flow forecast into your Business Plan. Show how you will manage your cash-flow. It is very important to put this in your Business Plan as getting it wrong will lead your business to an early death.

 **tip**

Don't try and trick the tax authorities. You will regret it forever, and it will cost you a fortune.

tip

Every pound spent is a pound less profit: spend very, very wisely.

… but you have to speculate to accumulate. So before spending every pound ask how much money this pound will make. And if I spent it another way, would that make me more money?

How financially strong is your business?

In our Business Plan we predict lots of financial figures, yet how certain are we they are realistic? Well, we can get quotations for some of our expenditure, e.g. professional fees, rent, etc. We can look at the jobs market and look at staff costs. And if we're lucky we can try and get some indicative orders for our products/services. So we can do our best. And lenders will appreciate this.

Ultimately we can offer no guarantees. And much will remain speculative until we begin trading. So how can we add greater certainty? If we cannot add any more certainty into our Plan we

What does it show?   How you plan to spend money and plan for expected sales.

What to look for: That sales figures are realistic and believable and, where possible, supported by evidence.
That income exceeds outgoings. Sounds obvious, but many people seem to think some sort of 'magic money' keeps businesses going.
Different to a cash-flow, this doesn't directly link the time of the cash coming in and going out, just months' and accumulative total sales and expenses.
That the Accumulative Actuals figures looks good, e.g. in just looking at one month, a small loss may seem nothing, but 10 months of small losses creep up to be a big loss.

	Month 1				Month 2				Month 3				… up to Month 12		
	Budget	Actual	% Target	Acc. % to date	Budget	Actual	% Target	Acc. % to date	Budget	Actual	% Target	Acc. % to date	Budget	Actual	% Target
Sales															
Product/Service A	£1,000	£1,275	128%		£1,000	£1,950	195%		£1,000	£1,545	155%		£1,500		
Product/Service B	£1,500	£767	51%		£3,000	£2,256	75%		£3,000	£3,245	108%		£3,500		
Product/Service C	£95	£95	100%		£95	£0	0%		£95	£350	368%		£395		
Total sales	£2,595	£2,137	82%	82%	£4,095	£4,206	103%	95%	£4,095	£5,140	126%	106%	£5,395		
			Sales above 100% is good												
Costs															
Fixed costs															
Rent	£500	£500	100%		£500	£500	100%		£500	£500	100%		£500		
Salaries/wages	£2,100	£2,100	100%		£2,100	£2,100	100%		£2,100	£2,100	100%		£2,100		
Car costs	£250	£157	63%		£250	£330	132%		£250	£157	63%		£250		
Marketing	£75	£295	393%		£75	£65	87%		£75	£295	393%		£75		
Professional fees	£50	£50	100%		£50	£50	100%		£50	£50	100%		£50		
Insurance	£50	£50	100%		£50	£50	100%		£50	£50	100%		£50		
Interest payments	£95	£254	267%		£95	£145	153%		£95	£254	267%		£95		
Variable costs															
Raw materials	£300	£350	117%		£300	£500	167%		£300	£350	117%		£300		
Overtime	£450	£750	167%		£450	£950	211%		£600	£750	125%		£450		
Etc.															
Total expenditure	£3,870	£4,506	116%	116%	£3,870	£4,690	121%	119%	£4,020	£4,506	112%	117%	£3,870		
			Expenditure above 100% is not good												
Monthly profit	−£1,275	−£2,369	186%		£225	−£484	−215%		£75	£634	845%		£1,525		

Cash-flow Forecast

What does it show? It shows the flow of 'cash' in and out of the business.

What to look for: If the cash balance goes negative, you've run out of money and unless you can find more money, you are in trouble.
A big positive cash balance shows you are doing well and will be attractive to banks and investors.

	Month 1	Month 2	Month 3	Month 4	Month 5	Month 6	Month 7	Month 8	Month 9	Month 10	Month 11	Month 12	...or could be weeks or even days		
Cash in															
Cash in hand	7,000	5,410	4,365	3,120	1,715	0	0	0	0	0	0	0	0	0	0
Cash sales	550	650	650	700	700	700	700	800	1,000	1,200	800	800	800	800	800
Cash from paid invoices	100	700	800	600	1,000	1,000	1,000	1,000	1,000	1,800	1,500	1,500	2,000	2,000	2,000
Total Cash in	7,650	6,760	5,815	4,420	3,415	1,700	1,700	1,800	2,000	3,000	2,300	2,300	2,800	2,800	2,800
Cash out															
Salaries	800	1,200	1,500	1,500	1,500	1,000	1,000	1,000	1,000	1,000	1,000	1,000	1,000	1,000	1,000
Materials/goods purchased	750	500	500	500	500	750	750	750	750	750	750	750	750	750	750
Rent	400	400	400	400	400	400	400	400	400	400	400	400	400	400	400
Travel	75	75	75	75	75	75	75	75	75	75	75	75	75	75	75
Telephones/internet	40	40	40	40	40	40	40	40	40	40	40	40	40	40	40
Insurance	150	150	150	150	150	150	150	150	150	150	150	150	150	150	150
Bank charges	25	30	30	40	175	30	30	45	45	45	45	45	45	45	45
Etc.															
Total Cash out	2,240	2,395	2,695	2,705	2,840	2,445	2,445	2,460	2,460	2,460	2,460	2,460	2,460	2,460	2,460
Cash balance	5,410	4,365	3,120	1,715	575	−745	−745	−660	−460	540	−160	−160	340	340	340

Month 5: 575 — Money runs out – the end! Inject cash or use bank overdraft.

Month 10: 540 — Back in the black, this month just!

Profit & Loss Account

What does it show?   A summary of how you spent your money and what
                         money you received over the past 12 months.

What to look for: The 'bottom line' of the P&L shows if you made a profit or
                         a loss in the past 12 months.
                         Breakdown allows us to see where the money went in the
                         year.

	Expenditure	Income
Turnover (sales income)		£350,000
Less cost of sales (cost of making the profit)	£200,000	
Gross profit		£150,000
Less expenditure		
Rent	6,000	
Salaries/wages	35,000	
Car costs	3,000	
Marketing	1,500	
Professional fees	725	
Insurance	575	
Interest payments	2,750	
Etc.		
Sub-total of expenditure	49,550	
Net profit		100,450

Balance Sheet

What does it show? A 'snapshot' of what the business owns (assets) and what it owes (liabilities).

What to look for:

That assets are larger than liabilities.

That a business with significant assets (with limited liabilities) is valuable (as the new owner could sell them) and is good to lend to or invest in.

When liabilities exceed assets, the business is technically insolvent and may be in serious trouble.

A Balance Sheet is a 'snapshot' of the value of that business on the day specified, and is not about the future.

This is a very simple Balance Sheet. They can be complex and need an accountant to interpret them.

Rules for compiling a Balance Sheet vary between countries.

Current Assets		
Cash at bank and in hand	£5,000	
Stock	£12,000	
Trade debtors (what customers owe you)	£4,000	
Equipment	£21,000	
Fixed assets	£75,000	
Intangible assets (e.g. IP, brand, etc.)	£20,000	
Total assets	£137,000	
Current liabilities (and falling due within 12 months)		
Trade creditors (what you owe people)	£5,000	
Bank loan	£7,000	
Long-term debt (over 12 months)	£57,000	
Total liabilities	£69,000	
Net assets	£68,000	
Shareholder equity	£68,000	

can test it to check the strength of our financial predictions. This is a process known as sensitivity analysis.

We do this by changing one of the figures in our budget, one at a time, and seeing how much this affects our P&L. It is best to also do this with our cash-flow forecast to see how that is affected, i.e. do we run out of cash sooner or later?

The easiest way to do this is to use a spreadsheet on the computer, as changing one thing will then change all the calculations (if we have set it up using formulas).

Best to play around and see what happens. One commonly-quoted test is to 'halve your income and double your costs'. How does the business look now?

What we are seeking to establish here is how sensitive your Plan is to changes, i.e. if you change one parameter by a small amount, does it tumble you into loss? If so, not so good. Or, can you changes things a lot and still keep cash/profit in the business? A good thing. Also work out what things are most sensitive – we need to manage them particularly closely.

work out what things are most sensitive – we need to manage them particularly closely

brilliant tip

Get a good accountant. Full stop.

Where to turn for financial advice

This is where a good accountant earns their money. For most small business owners managing the financial side is a chore. It is further complicated by the need to do certain things all the time and also to keep up to date with finance/tax legislation. A good accountant should:

- Help you plan your business – specifically the financial side.
- Tell you what to do in money management/record-keeping on a day-to-day basis and help you set up a system. Of course they may charge for this service, but at least you'll then know how and won't need to pay the accountant in the future.
- Use their experience to help you spot financial warning signs/danger signals that you may be heading into trouble.
- Help you plan to grow.
- Prepare or help you prepare your annual figures and your annual tax returns.
- Keep themselves and therefore you up to date with changes in financial regulations, etc.
- Provide impartial advice about different borrowing options/lenders.
- Be willing to negotiate on your behalf with banks, debtors, tax authorities, etc.

An accountant is not there to be your new best friend, they are a professional adviser; but they must be someone you can trust and rely upon.

It isn't possible to go over all the critical details of accountants, finance, tax, etc. in this book. And it is too important to get wrong, both legally and for your financial security. From this point on in the life of your new business, take advice from a good accountant.

The key question: how much will it cost? Estimate around £100 to £150 per hour for a good accountant appropriate for a small business start-up. But always ask. People often say they are embarrassed to ask an accountant (equally a lawyer, etc.) for their hourly rate or fee for a particular task. Look at it this way, an accountant themselves would never ask for work to be done without asking the price and getting a written quotation – part of the culture of being a good accountant! And actually, by asking them how much they charge, they will probably increase their respect for you as a businessperson who is on top of managing their organisation.

If your business is of sufficient size, say 10 to 20 staff or so, you might consider employing your own accountant full time to work in the business. For a smaller business, you might employ a part-time accountant – and there are often retired/semi-retired people or those with family responsibilities who will take on this role. They often have lots of experience but just don't want to work full time.

And whilst we are on the subject of hiring a good accountant – as appropriate, seek advice from other professionals, e.g. lawyers, intellectual property lawyers, health and safety consultants, insurance advisors, etc. Yes, these people will charge and it will cost you, but nowhere near what it will cost you if you get these things wrong …

brilliant recap

- There is no such thing as not-for-profit or a non-profit organisation. Mr Micawber was right – we must earn more than we spend.
- Be clear about how you will make money (the business model). We can't live on thin air and only money will do.
- Cash-flow is the silent killer: keep on top of it. Show your cash-flow forecast and your policy for managing cash-flow.
- A Profit & Loss budget for the first 12 months along with a summary of the first three years is critical. You and your lenders/investors will want to know how much money you will make.
- Get yourself a good accountant. It is worth the money. Use them from now on.

CHAPTER 6

Funding your business

'Acquaintance, n.: A person whom we know well enough to borrow from, but not well enough to lend to.'

Ambrose Bierce, *The Devil's Dictionary*, US author and satirist (1842–1914)

I t costs money to start a business. And I don't want to be the slayer of dreams here but the romantic notion that individuals start with less then nothing and build a successful business ... well, it does happen but don't count on it. The bottom line is that a business turns a smaller amount of money into a larger amount of money; so we need some money to start with.

Sources of funding

A number of sources of money are available:

- Your own money.
- Your personal borrowings, e.g. personal overdraft, loans, credit cards.
- Loans from family and friends.
- Your company borrowings, e.g. personal overdraft, loans, credit cards.
- Grants.
- Investors, e.g. business angels, venture capitalists.

Each has good and bad points and each tends to work in certain circumstances.

Before considering which ones are right for you (later in this chapter) we should look at some options.

Your own money in the form of savings is cheap (no interest to pay) and you only have to convince yourself to invest in your business. The upper limit is simply the limit of your savings.

Personal borrowings refer to money you borrow from banks and other lenders in your name that you then give/lend to your business. These can be from very low amounts to the limit of your personal borrowing capacity that is, in turn, usually related to your borrowing ability based upon your previous salary. It could be unsecured debt, e.g. credit cards or small personal loans, or secured debt, e.g. a personal loan or mortgage secured on your personal property. Typically these are borrowings that you will pay back over a period of a few months to a few years.

It is worth highlighting at this point that your personal ability to borrow changes dramatically for the worse when you move from employed to self-employed or to new business owner. As an employed person with a regular salary (and a good credit record) you are a safe person for a bank to lend to. As the owner of a new business, you may have become the least safe person and they will more likely say no to a loan. So, and lots of people will likely shout at me for saying this, but here goes, before you give up your job consider building up a nice line of credit, overdraft, some credit cards, etc. Don't use them or use them just enough to keep the facility, but retain them for emergency use. Once you have started your business you may not get this credit again for some years.

> your personal ability to borrow changes dramatically for the worse when you move from employed to self-employed or to new business owner

It is also worth organising your mortgage arrangements/borrowings/house moves before you leave employment. Not doing so was a mistake I made. Once I wanted to extend our mortgage within the first year of a new business. But our lender had a rule that said they would only lend to self-employed people who could present three years of accounts. So despite our excellent payment records, we could not extend the mortgage. This was a big name high-street lender and this was a common restriction amongst high-street lenders. Fortunately we found a broker who found a lender that specialised in mortgages for the self-employed and we got around that situation. A close call but don't make the same mistake; sort out the mortgage before you start your business.

Borrowing from family and friends may be low cost (although some may charge you interest) and may be over a fixed or a flexible duration (so potentially could be easy).

Company borrowings have similar sources as personal borrowings but are based upon the borrowing potential of your business (rather than your personal borrowing potential). And such potential will be assessed by the information in your Business Plan. In providing such business borrowings, lenders will consider what you will be using the money for; will it be for general running expenses (providing cash-flow) or will it be to purchase assets such as business premises? In the latter case, as their money is going into something tangible, and therefore could be sold in the future, they are more likely to provide funding. Also banks, and other lenders, will sometimes lend money to the business if the owners/directors provide some personal form of security, e.g. your house, to secure the debt. Where the bank takes some form of security and are lending larger sums they are likely to take a stronger interest in how your business is being run.

Grants originate from all sorts of places, e.g. your local council, central government, charities, etc and are usually available to support individuals in starting a business (a very good thing to encourage as it helps the local and the country's economy). Each will have their own criteria for applicants and some funding will be a grant whilst others might be in the form of a loan. Some are open to all, some to specific groups and some to those who cannot access business finance elsewhere. If it is free money – what are you waiting for? I once received £300 from my local council to go towards professional services: so we spent £600 with a local company who designed our logo and printed our first letterhead paper and business cards.

Investor finance is where an individual (business angel) or an organisation (venture capitalist (VC)) will put money into your business in return for owning a share of it. This is usually for big amounts of money (especially for VCs) and usually such investors will only become involved once you have demonstrated a strong track record or likely the business is already generating profits (but a business angel may help a start-up). At some point in the future the investor will want to recover their money by selling their part of the business. Whilst they are involved they are of course a part-owner of the business and so it is not wholly yours.

Your choice of funding

 **timesaver**

Get as many credit facilities in place before you leave your job!

Choosing which source of funding (or combination of sources) is right for you depends on two questions:

- Which ones are open to you?
- Which ones do you feel comfortable with?

Many people starting their own business frequently say one of the most important reasons for doing so is 'to have more freedom' (or some similar point of view). So when considering financing your business, how much of that sense of freedom do you wish to keep? If the answer is 'all of it' then you should stick to just using your own money. For as soon as we begin using other people's money (and of course using other people's money is always attractive) they start to have some say in how we run the business. Clearly if we have investors, they will own a part of it and have a direct say in decisions. But where the bank or others lend to the business they also have a say, be it directly in decisions or indirectly, because they have the right to remove their lending at their discretion. If they don't believe in or don't like the direction the business is going they can remove their money. So not only will we be competing with our competitors, we will have to put effort into 'fighting' with the bank. Sometimes even 'friends and family' start to have opinions about how you are running the business 'with their money' and this can lead to friction in previously harmonious relationships. If you want to avoid such potential conflict, stick to using your own money.

But we face a challenge in that we often don't have enough money ourselves and indeed many relatively new businesses go bust because they run out of finance before they have the time to get established (see cash-flow in Chapter 5). So frequently we do have to access money from elsewhere.

For a new business and a new business owner, accessing investor funding may be a challenge. Not impossible, but a challenge. Any business is a risky venture so the number of investors for this type of operation is limited. A new business with a new business owner, even more so. Throw into the equation an innovative product and service (that may change the world but there is

for a new business and a new business owner, accessing investor funding may be a challenge

no competitor yet to compare it with) and we have the riskiest venture of all. There are, however, still investors who diversify their investor activities and will have some money available for such speculative start-ups.

If you are an individual with a track record in the industry and/ or you have successfully run a start-up then your record will likely speak for itself and business angels and venture capitalists may well invest in you.

The other issue about venture capitalists in particular is that they usually look to make bigger investments (probably in the millions), so these are more commonly in established, growing businesses rather than new businesses.

Grants tend to be smaller so will likely form part of your funding, along with your personal money, commonly supplemented with borrowings, typically from a bank. The first issue to consider is whether you borrow personally or borrow as a business. Now there are likely to be tax implications here and this is a key point to discuss with your accountant. But aside from these issues we can consider what you feel comfortable with. As you are likely to be a sole trader, a partner or a limited company. Most people prefer to be a limited company and keep business and personal money separate. And potentially (but talk to your accountant as this is complex) if your business loses money you could shut it down, leaving debts, but your personal assets would remain safe. Knowing this, banks like to lend their money in situations where there are some assets that can be recovered if the worst happens, so an effectively empty company isn't something banks feel comfortable with. It is probable the owners/directors of the company may need to borrow the money personally and then lend it to the company. Once the company is established with good money flow then banks may be more willing to lend. Conversely, as a sole trader or partner your business and personal affairs are much closer together. Banks will then see the two sides of your life as being much more closely linked and it may be easier for them to recover money from your personal assets, so they may be more willing to lend.

Banks can seize your personal assets if at any time you have secured your business debts against your personal assets. If you agree to the bank using your home as security, they can take it away easily.

One of your most important decisions to make is whether you offer the bank your home as security for your business borrowing. It will likely make it much easier to borrow money as it is a virtual win-win for the bank; if you do well in your business you pay back the money (the bank gets its money) and if you do not do so well the bank can seize your home and sell it to recover its money (the bank gets its money). Why wouldn't they lend? (although it is more complex than that). The issue here for you to consider is that when your business has money troubles it will worry you. How can I pay the staff? How can I pay the tax? Etc. But if your home is secured against it you don't just face losing your business but losing your home too. Another way of looking at it is if you take a journey on a ship, it will carry a lifeboat, just in case the ship sinks. Your home is effectively your lifeboat, so if your business goes down, you have somewhere to go. And if you really are broke then you can always choose to sell your home and recover some money. The big difference is whether your bank chooses to sell your house or whether you choose.

Whatever you decide, one thing to consider is that banks don't like to be the only lender and like to share the risk. Put yourself in the position of lender; someone comes to you with a brilliant idea and wants you to put in some money. You naturally ask how much they are putting in and they say, 'Nothing'. How convinced would you be of their idea? Would you invest? No. If it is a good idea they would be risking some of their money. And it is the same with banks. If your idea is so sound (and it must be to start a business with it) why wouldn't you 'put your money where your mouth is'? Even on assets such as property you may find the bank will only lend up to 50% to 60% of the property value; you must find the rest.

 **tip**

Remember, a bank is a business and its legitimate business goal is to make money from its customers, i.e. you!

How much funding do I need?

Enough. Sounds flippant but that is the answer. Seeking too much funding will not be an attractive option as people reading your Business Plan will see that it is not financially efficient, i.e. that you are wasting money, buying things you don't need, and ultimately may not be making enough profit. Beware largess. You will meet people (who usually don't have businesses!) who know you can offset some of your costs thereby reducing your tax bill (true) and therefore it is tax efficient to buy an expensive new car (not always). Tax efficiency isn't the point here, you are a start-up and may not even pay much tax. The point is that the car has to be paid for upfront or each month out of your income and such extravagance is to be avoided in the early days. The other aspect is that as businesspeople we are expected to be sensible, even clever, with money so if the reader sees largess in our Business Plan that will lead them to doubt our competence, and make it less likely they will lend to us.

 **tip**

About this car issue, I suspect you may not be convinced. The 'I need a nice car to impress the clients' syndrome is usually just an excuse to blow too much money in a nice car dealership, and the business will pay! Remember 'needs' and 'wants' – which one are you following? If you are in a status market, and only if, buy a good brand of car, buy a five-year-old one and put a private plate on it. Remember, truly wealthy people are happy to drive an old banger; they have nothing to prove.

If we are seeking larger-scale funding from investors remember that they will be seeking a balance between the amount of money they put in and the amount they will get back over time. So if we ask for too much in the first place then their rate of return may, by comparison with less initial outlay, look smaller and therefore make it an unattractive investment.

Does that mean we should ask for the absolute minimum possible? No. Chances are that our business will not conform to our Business Plan in the early stages; it is likely we will sell less and spend more. Now an experienced person reviewing our Business Plan, say a banker or potential investor, will know this to be the reality and they may see that our business does not have enough money in it to get it going and to make it viable. Most businesses go bust in the first year because they run out of money. So there is no point in backing a losing horse, and they will not lend us the money.

> chances are that our business will not conform to our Business Plan in the early stages

The key is to strike a balance, asking for enough money to be realistic but avoiding appearing wasteful.

Ultimately, how you finance your business is your decision, but this is one area where seeking objective advice is critical.

Approaching people for funding

Here a good accountant should be of significant value. Not only in helping you prepare your Business Plan but in helping you identify potential funders and hopefully helping to make introductions to these people. Most local accountants know most of the managers in the local banks and those who have been in business a while will have a network of business angels and/or venture capitalists they work with.

Once the introductions have been made the approach is based upon the quality of the Business Plan. Specifically, the main part of it is about demonstrating to lenders/investors that your business is worth investing in and this is done by addressing the key questions we focus upon in the Executive Summary, e.g.:

● What is the need (to which your business is the answer) and how strong is this need (market)?

● How will your business be successful in addressing this need?

● How much money will your business make?

● Do they believe in you and your team having the ability to be successful in competing in this market?

● Is your Business Plan realistic?

And because this is about approaching funders who, by their nature, are numbers people, the financial side of your Business Plan needs to be realistic. But they are also good at the bigger picture so we shouldn't just focus upon the numbers.

Putting funding into your Business Plan

Your funding needs to be described in the Business Plan in full. Most of the people who read it will know a business has to be adequately funded so it is important to present this in words.

It is also necessary to show funding coming into the financial budgets of your Plan. It should appear as numbers in your Profit & Loss, and in your cash-flow.

 **action**

Present

(i) a full description of how your business will be funded; and

(ii) show this funding in your Profit & Loss, cash-flow forecasts and balance sheet.

---

brilliant recap

- To make money we need money, so your business will need start-up funding from somewhere.
- It is natural that potential funders will want to see you putting some of your money into your business. They want you to share the risk and to be financially/emotionally locked-in.
- When looking for funding remember the key questions investors will be asking.
- Look to adequately fund the business.
- But think carefully about putting in all your money/assets, especially your home. It is important to have a lifeboat.

CHAPTER 7

The people side of your Plan

'The person who knows how will always have a job. The person who knows why will always be his boss.'

Diane Ravitch, quoted in *Quotable Business*, by Louis E. Boone

I t is now important in writing the Business Plan to return to some of the internal dimensions of the business. And in particular, the people to run it. A business is made up of people so how do we organise and manage this important element? And, importantly, how do we highlight this in the Business Plan?

You are the boss

When we are seeking lenders/investors, three questions arise in their minds:

1 Is there a market?
2 Does the business have the products/services to win?
3 Does the business have the people to make it happen?

Particularly, does the business have the people in charge who can make it happen? Opportunity can lie nearby but unless we have the people who can manage/lead and put it all in place, it will remain an untaken opportunity. So it is very important to get the boss and the management team right and to show they are right in the Business Plan.

Perhaps the first and most significant change for you, the new business owner, is that you are now in charge. For many this is something they are very much looking forward to, for others it is not something they consider in the beginning.

For most people, it will be different to other work. Even for those people who have been managers, they've been within an organisation so they were managing within a network. Now it all stops with you. Some people will love this, some will find it daunting, but in the beginning it will probably be challenging so we should prepare for it. Some aspects we should consider are listed below.

In a small business the boss doesn't get to sit in an office and simply manage ... in a small business the boss does everything – we should prepare to be hands-on

In a small business we might think we will all be friends ... yes, we want to have very good relationships and friendships, but keep a little distance as you are still the boss.

Some people may appear to be anti-boss ... but they still want a boss.

It may be a group of people, who get on ... but when something serious goes wrong, they will all turn to you for the answer.

Boss = leadership + management ... these are different things.

'Management is doing things right; leadership is doing the right things.'

Peter Drucker

So what is the distinction between management and leadership? Drucker's thought helps us here. Imagine you are a manager in a firm and you have to organise the processing of paperwork associated with people applying for a licence. People get hold of the form, complete it, post it to you, you open it, have it checked, have it scanned for a record, put it into a file and send it to a colleague in another location. You do it magnificently. For every year for three years you have improved operational efficiency and are processing more forms with the same resources. Excellent, good management. Here, a 'leader' would say, 'Why?' Why do people need to apply for this licence? Why do people have to use a paper form (that we scan)? Why don't we ask/allow people to do it electronically and save us handling paper/scanning? Good leadership.

Now there may be reasons why things are done in a certain way but the leader is there to challenge, to question why. If our competitors are leading in this way, they may be improving their efficiency and in doing so they may be gaining competitive advantage over us.

> there may be reasons why things are done in a certain way but the leader is there to challenge, to question why

 **action**

For your Business Plan, compile and present evidence of your experience in being a manager and/or leader. A two-page CV for the Business Plan appendix is a good idea but in the Plan itself highlight relevant experience, knowledge, qualifications, membership of professional societies, etc. Present reasons why you will adjust well to the position of being the boss.

Also include the experience, CVs, etc. of other key staff. The strength of the team is important in the minds of the lenders.

The key jobs

Now we have the boss covered, we can consider our business in its component parts and think about how these will be organised and who will be responsible for delivering what.

- We need something to sell.
  - Either develop our own products/services – so we need some sort of 'new product development' capability.
  - Or we buy-in products/services – in which case we need some sort of 'purchasing capability'.
- We need to make the products/services.
  - So we need some 'production people'.
- We will not make any money unless people know our business and our products/services exist.
  - So we need some marketing and salespeople.
- We need a means of getting the product/service to the customer.
  - That means distribution channel.
  - That means 'distribution people'.
- We want customers to be able to pay us with money.
  - Finance people are therefore really important.
- We need someone who can ensure all theses things and people work together.
  - So an operations manager will be good.
- And finally someone to lead us into the future.
  - A leader.

So does that mean that every business has to have at least seven people? No. But all businesses do need to perform the functions of seven people.

For the one-person business, you will have to divide your time seven ways: you have to create the products/services, make them, sell them, deliver them, organise everything and lead your business into the future. (No surprise then that small business owners work more hours than employed staff.) Further, not all these tasks earn you money! For example, a lawyer might charge per hour but only when working on the client's business; the client won't pay for that lawyer to sell. So the costs of all these activities have to be covered in the prices we charge our customers. You will have to decide how your time will be divided between the tasks and, importantly, make this clear in the Business Plan.

 **action**

Show how you will divide your time. And the time of staff. Does this give you enough time to make money?

There are concerns that the business will be unbalanced and once one part of the operation goes down, the remainder will likely go down. Some common scenarios are given in brilliant questions and answers below.

brilliant questions and answers

Q **Problem**: Selling lots, but production cannot make all that is being sold.

A **Solution**: Increase production capacity or increase prices to reduce demand and make more money out of selling less.

Q **Problem**: Delivering lots of work but no one is sending out the invoices (surprisingly common!).

A **Solution**: Employ someone to do the invoices or deliver less so you can do the invoices.

Q **Problem**: No point in spending lots of time marketing 'old' products/services that are out of date that no-one wants to buy.

A **Solution**: Develop some new products/services.

until we have sufficient work to keep a person fully occupied that may not be worth it. So what other options do we have?

Now even the one-person business is in fact not alone, because in this position we can buy-in people to help us. We can hire them but until we have sufficient work to keep a person fully occupied that may not be worth it. So what other options do we have?

- We can hire professionals, e.g. an accountant, good for important things but perhaps expensive for routine issuing of invoices.

- We can hire part-time people either on a regular ten hours a week or an 'as and when' basis. There are a surprising number of talented, experienced people who will take on such work. Often they don't want to run their own business or be a full–time employee, but would like to do something and earn extra money. For example, retired/semi-retired people who have lots of experience are pleased to earn more but equally often enjoy passing on their knowledge and experience. People with child-care responsibilities, especially if you can be flexible with their hours, are another (often under-utilised) talent and resource.

- There are telephone answering services so calls to your business number goes to them and they answer in your name. A nice service, as it makes us look like a substantial business and always gives a nice welcome to those calling us. Virtual secretarial services are available.

- Your local business school/university/college will likely have business students who will really welcome the opportunity to work in a real business, on real business ideas as part of their course or simply to gain some real work experience.

- You can coerce your family and friends to do it for nothing; an obviously attractive option but maybe more a temporary solution rather than a permanent one.

 **action**

You want these people to be reliable so expect to pay them properly; have
a proper business relationship with them from the start.

As we start a larger business or grow our business we need more
people. We need not have one person wearing multiple hats but
can start to organise so that individuals start to focus on specific
areas. It may be that one person still does more than one thing
but perhaps they have fewer things to think about. At what point
this process begins depends on our business and our financial
position, and it will cost more but then again, allowing for people
with specific expertise to focus on that strength should pay divi-
dends in the longer term. Some examples include the following:

- If an individual can earn £1,000 a day giving advice, why
  stop them to make them sit in the office issuing their
  invoices?
- Can we find a way to stop the best salesperson spending
  time sorting out problems in the factory?
- Why is the boss spending time chasing customers to pay?

Are there any rules of thumb to guide us? Probably.

- In the beginning we may have little work, so even if there is
  only one of us we still have time to do everything.
- Once we begin delivering/earning, then almost immediately
  we can benefit from some administration and someone to
  answer our telephone.
- If we have a significant number of staff, especially part-
  timers/casuals, e.g. a hotel or shop, organising them takes
  a lot of time so someone managing the staff becomes
  important.

- Once we reach a few invoices a week and/or we are employing staff, someone to manage the money becomes very important.

- If we are running a web-based business, someone to manage the web is probably necessary from Day 1.

- Once we get to say ten or so staff, a full-time finance manager is probably a necessity.

- Once we get to 50 or so staff, we will probably need a finance director.

 **action**

Show how you will ensure the key activities are adequately covered. Include specific people with their backgrounds to demonstrate to yourself and lenders/ investors that you have the right people and you will create the right team.

Growing the business

'Be not afraid of growing slowly; be afraid only of standing still.'

Chinese proverb

You might be of the view that you aren't planning to become a big business. Maybe you think there is only room for a small business. Or maybe you want 'freedom' and keeping it small will mean you have total control over your domain. And there is a lot to say for that view – you should run the business, the business should not run you. I recall meeting a gentlemen who had 12 staff in a previous business but in his new one there were none, and his annual turnover would never be above the compulsory VAT threshold as he didn't want to bother with that either.

However, we should consider one important aspect; our costs grow. Year on year, things become more expensive; our staff will want a pay rise, our suppliers will be seeking an increase in their prices, our customers will want reduced prices … suddenly it's like being a sardine in a can. The way we survive these crushing pressures is by growing our income and, in doing so, growing our business. Maybe fast, maybe slowly, but at a very minimum we need to grow by at least the same as the inflation of our costs (at the time of writing, maybe 5% a year). If we don't we are squeezed more and more. If our income remains the same, our costs go up, so we make a little less profit. So our income remains the same, and our costs increase more, so a little less profit … and then … there comes a time where our costs are the same as our income … and one more jump and our costs are over our income … and we are now losing money. This is how businesses die. And changing a business, in this case increasing income, will take money (changing anything always does) and once we are making a loss, we have no money. So if nothing else and for no other reason, we must grow a little.

And at the opposite end of the scale investors, especially business angels and venture capitalists, will want us to grow a lot. Why? Because a growing business is a potentially valuable business and the investors need a way to recover their money. If you have significantly grown the business it will be much more valuable when you come to sell part or all of it.

> if you have significantly grown the business it will be much more valuable when you come to sell part or all of it

brilliant action

Present your plans for growth (or otherwise). Give the reader a clear impression on how big you will be. How quickly you plan to get there. And how you plan to get there.

Can you grow?

One of the considerations for growing a business is, can it be grown? Or in the jargon, is it scalable? Think about a factory that makes fruit drinks. The work is relatively non-specialised so there are many staff who could be recruited and trained to do the job. So with more sales, the factory can produce more product. The only limitation is the size of the factory and if we have strong sales growth then it is likely we can borrow the money to obtain a bigger factory. The business can be scaled up, it can be grown. Now consider a one-person consultancy business, where the owner has unique knowledge of a particular industry. Once that person has sold all their time, how will they expand? Only by finding another person with similar knowledge (so not many to choose from?) or finding individuals with knowledge in related areas into which the business can expand. So the business can be grown but it will be more difficult to grow. And it is unlikely to achieve the sorts of growth rate that investors, particularly venture capitalists, will look for.

 **action**

Related to your 'Plans for growth', it is important that you say how you will scale up the business. And what will the limiting factors be, e.g. staff, market size, licence agreements, etc. The reason for doing this is that it will demonstrate to the reader your appreciation of this key issue.

Family business

Whilst we consider growing our business it is important to consider the special case of family businesses. Family businesses are different, principally because we encounter a greater range of emotions. And these emotions make it difficult to manage the business in the objective ways we should.

Common family business issues include the following:

- You cannot get away from the business as you talk about it at work and then talk about it at home.

- You may start out family-only but then as you grow you may need to hire non-family members of staff/managers.

- You have two types of employees – family and non-family – and it can be difficult to make both groups happy.

- Family members may have positions within the firm, even though they lack the skills necessary for the job.

- Non-family members, even in senior positions, may feel out of it, because the big decisions are taken over Sunday lunch – when they are not there.

But of course if you can make it work, who better than your family to work with?

So if you are planning a family business, should you have something in your Plan referring to this point? Debatable, but I think the answer is yes. Thinking back to the beginning of this book and one of the advantages of business planning is that it forces us to think about important issues. Also, if you are looking for funding, lenders know family businesses are different so they will welcome evidence that you are thinking about these things.

 **action**

If you are to be a family business, write a short section highlighting the issues you may encounter and what actions you are taking to mitigate them.

 recap

● The people in the business are a critical success factor. Especially if you need lending or investments.

● The bigger the investment the more the investors will be looking at the team – can they deliver?

● There are a number of key functions within the business: leader, manager, sales and marketing, operations, distribution, and finance. We need good people in all these roles.

● If the business is smaller, or only you, these roles still need to be covered and you should make it clear how your/their time will be divided.

● How will you manage the people side of growing the business?

CHAPTER 8

Protecting your ideas

'Knowledge is power.'

Attributed to Sir Francis Bacon, English author, courtier and philosopher (1561–1626), Ferdowsi (940–1020) *and others*

Of one thing we can be certain; when our business becomes successful, other people will take note. And once they have taken note then they will want a piece of what we have. Obviously if we are successful we have that most important thing we seek in our Business Plan, a source of competitive advantage. But the very best we can have is a source of 'sustainable' competitive advantage, i.e. something that our competitors cannot take away even if they want to. In our business planning it is therefore important that we take steps to protect our business.

Do you know anything useful?

In the business you are planning, how important is knowledge? It is likely the answer is 'important'. But think further specifically what knowledge do you have that is vitally important? For there are sources of knowledge that may make or break your business and some examples are:

- The design of a product.
- Relationships with key clients.

- Specific knowledge about something, e.g. international corporate tax law.

Say you have developed a new mobile telephone that allows people to do things on the phone not possible before. You launch it and it becomes an instant success; you can barely keep up with the millions of sales. What will your competitors do? Buy one, work out how it works, make their own version and sell it at half the price (and they *can* sell it at half price, as you had to pay the research and development costs but they didn't). Is this allowed? Well, in general, yes and no. If we have taken no steps to protect the knowledge, design, etc of the phone, probably yes they can (how unfair is that?). But we can take steps to stop this; most of which is based around intellectual property rights (IPR) and protection, discussed in the next section.

Perhaps less obvious is the valuable knowledge hidden in relationships with key clients. Some customers have very little loyalty to you and will always shop around (usually those who buy on lowest price alone). But not all people are like this and indeed probably the majority are not, as they favour achieving value based upon a balance of price and relationships. So our getting on well, having trust and empathy and a 'connection' with clients becomes a source of advantage. Now if these relationships are with you, the owner, they are relatively secure. But if the relationships are with your staff, what happens if that staff member leaves? Potentially you lose a key client. Relationships as a source of advantage are common in professional services, e.g. law firms, accountants and consultancies, and in these sectors if one of your professionals leave they often take 'your' clients with whom they work with them to their new firm. It is possible to have contractual terms with you staff, e.g. perhaps they cannot start a business in competition with you in a certain time scale, location, etc. that may, to an extent, control your now ex-staff, but ultimately the client chooses who they want to work with and they may take a dim view of you if they feel you are seeking to dictate to them.

> the majority favour achieving value based upon a balance of price and relationships

Slightly distressingly there may be little we can ultimately do about this and we may have to live with it as a natural part of this type of market. However, one possible thing you could do is ensure you are involved in key relationships as well as your staff.

Specific knowledge may be one reason why you started your business in the first place; after all, why make money for someone else when you can use your knowledge to make money for yourself? But as we have seen in Chapter 7 that may hinder your ability to grow unless you can recruit others with similar or complementary specific knowledge. If you can, this is good and you can grow your business. An issue that arises though is what happens when one of these key knowledge-holders leaves? How do you fulfil your contracts/satisfy your customers if you can't give them the knowledge they need?

 **action**

Do a knowledge audit of your proposed business, i.e. what knowledge do you or will you possess in your business that is particularly valuable or even critical?

brilliant tip

If you are planning to buy a business that has strong, longstanding customer relationships, particularly with the owner, be very careful about not paying too much for it. With the original owner out of the business, some key customers may decide the reason to

▶

> automatically continue the relationship no longer exists and may (perhaps for the first time in years) look around for alternative suppliers.

 **action**

How will you stop your business losing important knowledge?

Protecting what you know

Having identified what is critical knowledge in our Business Plan, we need to consider how we can protect it.

In the case of product design, etc., we can use intellectual property laws to protect us. This is a complex area and no simple answers or 100% reliable solutions exist, so if your business is to be based upon critical knowledge, inventions, rights to sell a particular product, etc. then you must consult an intellectual property lawyer for advice.

Such IP-based businesses are increasingly common. One of the growth areas in recent years has been to start businesses that are based on the results of research coming from universities and other research organisations. The intellectual property rights resulting form the research results, say for a new design of electrical plug or a new food ingredient that makes one slim, will be licensed to a company (for a fee). And that company will have the exclusive rights to develop and sell that product. And because of the protection of the intellectual property legal system, it theoretically means another company cannot copy this product. So if no one else can sell it, the firm has no competitors – marvellous. But, and this is critical, your whole business potential and the value of your business is based upon the exclusive rights to this research so your IP protection must be as good as it possibly can be. This requires substantial effort and you must have excellent legal advice.

> your IP protection must be as good as it possibly can be

Perhaps the most prominent type of business based upon intellectual property is the pharmaceutical industry, where companies have legal rights (in this case a patent) to market and sell a specific chemical molecule (a drug). These exclusive rights last for a period of years, before other people can also market and sell the drug. In fact, whilst pharmaceutical companies are often very large, their value is usually based upon a relatively small number of patents for drugs which have or will have a very large market potential.

 **definition**

Intellectual Property (IP)
Results from the expression of an idea. So IP might be a brand, an invention, a design, a song or another intellectual creation. IP can be owned, bought and sold (UK Intellectual Property Office)

Broadly, there for fours types of intellectual property protection (based on UK Intellectual Property Office classifications):

1 Patents – legal rights to exclusivity for a product that may include process, design or invention.
2 Trade marks – symbols that distinguish goods in the market – e.g. a brand logo.
3 Designs – the design, including the look of something.
4 Copyright – an automatic right which applies when the work is fixed, i.e. written or recorded in some way.

From your knowledge audit (above), decide which forms of intellectual property protection you believe you need. This may seem like more legal work (and yes, it does cost) but there is nothing as soul-destroying as building a great business then to see someone else legitimately taking it because no one protected what could be protected. Only very recently a company I know of bought a business in the US, believing the US firm had the right to use certain valuable intellectual property, but it turned out the sellers did not declare a possible unresolved IP issue. So the US acquisition is now potentially worthless and it is being closed down. There is a legal challenge going to court and some money may be recovered, but for most people that is not the reason we go into business.

It is also worth pointing out there is, as yet, no *global* intellectual property system by which you can agree, for example, a patent that is then protected around the world. It is more a country-by-country approach. Also, the strength of the IP protection varies greatly from one country to another; in some it is strong, in others virtually non-existent and 'stealing' of ideas is commonplace.

IP rights are ok as long as you are willing to protect them from challenges. The unfortunate side to this area of law is that if someone appears to be infringing your IP it is for you to legally challenge them. This is a frustrating waste of your time and expensive and if, for example, it involves making a legal challenge in another country, it can be *very* expensive. It is possible to encounter firms (often big ones) that will deliberately steal your IP on the basis that they know you don't have enough money to be able to challenge them. A horrid and grotesquely unfair situation but something that might happen. This is most definitely *not* a reason not to use IP protection methods, but an illustration that they are not watertight. So sometimes other methods might be useful alongside to try and give practical protection.

Consider that you make technology consumer products in a very fast-developing market. You are the market leader and tend to be first with new innovation and new product. After a few months a competitor has a rival product out that is very similar to yours. But if you are the innovation leader, by the time they have launched their suspiciously similar product, you are ready to launch the next version. So your income is maintained by always being in the lead. Not a wholly reliable strategy but a possible path to give you a sense of additional security.

 **action**

How will you protect your knowledge and stop your business losing critical IP? What steps can you take to mitigate the loss of key people/knowledge?

Protecting your image

One of our goals is to build a presence in the market. And we achieve this through the good things we do and the reputation we build. That good reputation is in the hearts and minds of our existing and potential customers, its physical presence is in what those people can see – our building, our website, our logo, our branding, etc. So if, for example, you see the Marks & Spencer logo, you feel positive about M&S, you trust the firm, it stands for quality and fair prices, based upon their reputation and our experiences. Now what happens if another shop takes on a similar logo and names? It starts to cause confusion in the hearts and minds of our present and potential customers (and that is always a bad thing).

So just as when we set up our business we don't what to deliberately get too close to another identity, we don't want other new companies trying to steal our reputation by confusing the market. If someone does, we want the reassurance that as much about us has been protected as possible, e.g. brand names, logo, etc. and we will need to be willing to defend ourselves by repelling the attacker in the courts.

Putting knowledge in your Business Plan

a section on knowledge will surprise many people and impress others

Actually having a section in your Business Plan on knowledge will surprise many people and impress others, as they don't always expect this.

One group of people who will expect it are venture capitalists who back technology businesses. Their investment is often based upon your having full and exclusive protected rights to an invention/piece of knowledge. It must be very clear in your IP rights agreement which rights you have and which you don't. And the IP needs to be as well protected as possible.

 **action**

Write in your Business Plan statements about IP and what the important/critical knowledge is. Explain how you will protect this knowledge, included that embedded in your business, e.g. through relationships.

If your business is based upon IP rights, and especially if you are seeking external investment, you must have a very clear presentation of all the technical/legal details.

brilliant recap

- Knowledge is power.
- Sometimes, what we know is our only source of competitive advantage. We must protect it.
- For businesses based upon exploiting intellectual property, e.g. results from research in a patent, it is the only thing of value in the business. We must protect it.
- We should use formal systems to protect our knowledge.
- Sometimes, being first and being swift in the market also offers us knowledge advantage.

CHAPTER 9

How to reduce your Plan to two pages

The Executive Summary

'Always bear in mind that your own resolution to succeed is more important than any one thing.'

Abraham Lincoln, 16th president of US (1809–1865)

You will have laboured over producing the Plan so far and chances are it could be a reasonably sized document. Congratulations, and here is the bad news, you may be the only person who ever reads it! Read on ...

Goal

Our primary goal has been to convince other readers of the Plan. We've lived it, we know what is in the whole thing, and may even be slightly tired of it by now, so why do we need a summary to tell us what is in it? We don't.

But other people do. And whilst our Business Plan is very important in our life it may not be immediately important in their lives. In fact, it may be the third Business Plan they have read today. And by read, we don't mean read in full, we mean looked at quickly. This sounds, after all our work, slightly unfair, but that is one of the things we cannot readily change and have to live with. (When you are an investor perhaps you can make more time to read Business Plans sent to you.)

So the Executive Summary has only one goal:

● To get the reader interested in our business without reading the full Plan.

If we achieve this then they will either give us their support/ money (job done) or at least read the main part of the Business Plan.

Structure

The Executive Summary must focus on giving answers to the five crucial questions:

1 Is there an attractive market?

2 Does the business have the products/services to win?

3 Does the business have the people to make it happen?

4 How much money will the business make?

5 Where will the business go?

And these answers must clearly present a compelling case for setting up the business. Compelling, because if we have come this far and there isn't hard evidence for it then why are we persisting with this Business Plan? If the facts do not stack up, we should have put aside this idea and moved on to working on or developing the Plan for a different business.

> these answers must clearly present a compelling case for setting up the business

 **tip**

A great idea needs few words to convince people.

Therefore our Executive Summary should be:

● Between one and two pages long.

- In positive language (except when highlighting the risks, where we should use objective language).
- Start with a bold statement and end with a bold statement.
- Focus on addressing the five questions.
- Incorporate a synopsis of the whole Plan.
- Use 'numbers' to substantiate points.
- Draw upon the material from the main part of the Business Plan (i.e. do not put new or different information in here as when the reader looks at the main part of the Plan, different material will cause confusion).

Question 1 – Is there a market?

We should begin with a bold, attention-capturing statement that demonstrates the market opportunity. And we must make it good. To get a flavour of what impact feels like we can look at examples of the wise words of others.

- *'I have a dream.'* Martin Luther King Jr. Note that the man did not say, 'I have a potentially good idea.'

In literature, some writers put great store on the opening line of the novel; get that right and the reader will stay with you.

- 'There was no possibility of taking a walk that day' Charlotte Brönte, *Jane Eyre*

When we read lines like this they transport us, we are engaged. Flowery language may not quite fit with the objectives of the Business Plan but we need to create a compelling opening. And, ideally, this strong opening should given an impression of the market opportunity. Examples could be:

- 'The Brazilian economy is growing at 10% per year.'
- 'The World Bank estimates that cereal production needs to increase by 50% and meat production by 85% between 2000 and 2030 to meet demand.'

- 'The number of people aged 85 and over is projected to more than double over the next 25 years from 1.3 million in 2008 to 3.3 million by 2033.' (UK Office for National Statistics.)

What are the characteristics of these opening statements?

- They all point to a general market opportunity.
  - I.e. look, here we have an opportunity.
- They all highlight 'growth'.
  - Why launch a business in a falling market when you could pick a growing market?
- They give an impression of scale by including numbers.
  - Saying the market is growing is good, but is it growing by 1% or 20% per year? Obviously a big difference.
- The last two points have data sources included which adds confidence if they are reliable.
  - Our saying something positive in our Plan is to be expected but a respected authoritative source is more reliable (plus it demonstrates research on our part).
- They've all captured the attention of the reader.

Examples of strong opening statements:

'Government incentives for households to produce renewable energy is creating a market growing at 30% p.a, yet there is a significant shortage of firms to help householders. Our business can achieve turnover of £1m in two years.'

'A major high-street retailer has confirmed my products meet an unfulfilled need in the market. And if we were to go into production, they would place an order for 1,000 units at a price giving me a margin of 300%.'

Next, we have to move from a general to a more specific opportunity that adds further weight to the scale of the Plan. So if our business involves caring for older people in their homes then we would highlight the population growth figures (above) with, for example:

- Government statements emphasising a shift in policy from caring for patients in hospital to patients being treated in their homes.
- Independently published data and your own researched information about older people preferring to be cared for in their own homes.
- Figures (from wherever they can be gathered) indicating the financial size of the market.
- Etc.

Gather together pieces of supporting data that illustrate the nature of the opportunity and the scale and longevity of the potential market.

At this point in the Executive Summary, probably about a third of the way through, the reader should be convinced that not only is there an opportunity but an attractive opportunity, and one defined by trend, financial size and longevity.

> the reader should be convinced that there is an opportunity defined by trend, financial size and longevity

Question 2 – Does the business have the products/services to win?

So an opportunity is good (well, better than good) but it is only relevant here if we can now demonstrate that we have the products/services to capitalise on it. And this is our goal in this part of the Executive Summary – to show we can win in the market.

So here we should present information (remember this should be only half to one page):

- What is our product or service for this market?
- Show, with evidence, why it works in this market.
- Present your data to show, from your market research with your target segments, the positive response to your products/services.
- Who are the competitors?
- And critically, why will our products/services be better than any of the competitiors' products?

In this section, numbers are good. Where possible we need to 'prove' that our products/services stand a good chance of winning. Proving is, of course, difficult to do in any absolute sense but we must do all we can to build a case. Evidence that is useful here includes:

- Market research data from target customers.
- Independent analysis of your products – say, by a consultant experienced in this market.
- If your are selling your product to retailers, details of interviews with their buyers, category managers, etc.

But of course there is one sort of proof that really does count – a signed order. For some people this sounds unbelievable but in other markets it is almost the norm. Individuals leaving their firm to start their own business often have their old employer as their first customer, and they may have negotiated a contract. Often this happens when firms and public sector organisations decide to subcontract or outsource work; they know the person so are very happy to give it to them rather than have to search for someone else. Sometimes our business ideas come from talking to someone who says, 'We have real trouble finding anyone to do X'. Then it is possible to reply, 'So, if I could do X for you, would you give me the work?' If we start our business based on such an obvious but currently unfilled market demand then it is natural for customers to agree to support you. I do know someone who was looking to start a business and that is exactly what happened.

We have only half to one page for this so we cannot afford to waffle. That is why, where possible, numbers make sense here because they allow us to put over how strong are products/services are in only a few words.

Of course we can never prove our products will win so don't be put off if you don't have signed orders, but it is our time and money we are risking so we want convince ourselves as well as lenders.

Question 3 – Does the business have the people to make it happen?

In our Executive Summary we have demonstrated to the reader that there is a market, and it is attractive. And we have shown we have the products/services to win. But just because the market and the winning products/services exist doesn't mean we can make the business a success. Our final task is to convince our lenders that we are the people who can make this business work.

In the final half-page our goal is to convey the message that we are the right people to run this business. So here we detail the following:

> our goal is to convey the message that we are the right people to run this business

- Who will be running the business?
- Name the key individuals.
- What is their relevant experience?
- Why would they be good for our business?
- How committed are they to staying with our business?

Question 4 – How much money will the business make?

Ok, now onto the money side. It is likely the readers of this Plan are in some way offering us money, so they want to know if they will get it back. At this point we should prepare a financial summary and information to include:

- Expected income in the first year (based upon size of the market and market share we are likely to capture).
- Turnover per year for Years 1, 2 and 3.
- Gross and net profit expectations in each of these years.
- Repayment schedule for debt.
- Results of sensitivity analysis (see Chapter 5).
- Return on investment – for any investors.

Question 5 – Where will the business go?

By now the reader should be pretty certain of real potential and the only remaining issue to resolve is where the business will go. That is:

- How will you continue to grow the business? E.g.:
  - New products/services for this customer group?
  - Existing products for new customers?
- Will you grow the business organically or by merger/ acquisition?

Along with:

- Where will the business be in five years?

And:

- What are your personal plans?
  - Let the business grow forever? Or
  - Grow it to a certain point and sell it?

Our Executive Summary is virtually finished and only one task remains: to end with another attention-grabbing statement. Something that both summarises our proposition and highlights key points, e.g.:

This business will achieve first year sales of £500,000 at a gross profit of 80%, in a market forecast to grow at 20% p.a. over the next five years. By this time turnover will be £7m p.a. and the business will be number two in its main market. Return on investment will be 30% p.a.

Remember, we don't put all the details in the Executive Summary as the reader will have the whole Business Plan to refer to. Here it is enough to convince them that this is a sound Business Plan, even an exciting Business Plan, and to decide to read it in full. Indeed, if this Executive Summary is good enough, the reader will now be persuaded and will simply refer to the main part of the Plan to check the figures to substantiate the points made here.

Job done!

 **brilliant** recap

In the Executive Summary answer five key questions:

1   Is there an attractive market?

2   Does the business have the products/services to win?

3   Does the business have the people to make it happen?

4   How much money will the business make?

5   Where will the business go?

CHAPTER 10

Presenting your Business Plan

'Clarity of mind means clarity of passion, too; this is why a great and clear mind loves ardently and sees distinctly what it loves.'

Blaise Pascal, Mathematician and philosopher

...on paper

Clarity is key.

Chances are by the time we have come this far everything we have (or nearly everything) will be on paper. But it will probably need tidying up. So do this once, then put it aside for the weekend. After the break, re-read it and you will almost certainly find things to order, clarify or adjust.

Ask two friends to read it. One who is familiar with business to check it reads well from a business perspective. One who is good on language to check the grammar, spelling, tone, etc (my editors did this for me!). A friend rejected one potential estate agent to sell his house as the offer letter contained three typing mistakes. No one is likely to reject a cracking business idea just because your Business Plan has some bad spelling, but neither does it put them in a positive mood.

You have spent a lot of time on this Plan so do not scrimp on the final presentation. In marketing, some people have theories about the weight of the paper you use (heavier paper is better). You may have your own ideas about how you want to present your Business Plan on paper but if not, here are some suggestions:

- Heavier paper – say 90 or 100g/sm.

- A4 paper.

- Bright white paper.

- Glossier paper.

- Print in colour.

- Paper with a little colour or design in the margins often looks nice.

- Have it bound as something convenient that opens flat – some sort of spiral binder works well.

Many stationery/print shops do this whilst you wait and it costs only a few pounds. Just prepare your Plan in a standard word processing package and take it on a USB stick.

... in PowerPoint

First, do you really need to use PowerPoint? It is great for showing images, graphs, figures, etc. but sometimes it constrains you. Remember, your business does not yet exist so just like a service, one of the ways the potential customer (or here, lender) can buy into this proposition is to buy into the person selling it to them. And enthusiasm and passion are very seductive traits in a presenter. Use PowerPoint to *aid* you but not hold you back:

> enthusiasm and passion are very seductive traits in a presenter

- Keep the attention on you and not on the screen.

    - Being enthusiastic is the best way to do this.

- Do not read a script. You will sound dull. Instead, have a copy of your Business Plan to hand in case of any questions.

- Use no more than ten slides.

- Images are more powerful than words, e.g. instead of describing your target customers, use a picture.

- When there are many numbers, e.g. going through the Profit and Loss account, it is usually easier for people to read numbers.

  - Walk to the screen to point out the numbers then, when you have done this, pause, wait until the audience is looking at you and move away from the screen; their eyes will follow you.

- If the audience starts asking lots of good questions, sit down with them and continue the discussion – it is likely a sign they have bought into your Plan and have seen enough.

- Give the handout at the *end* of the presentation – you want them to engage with you and not a piece of paper.

- Make your opening and closing statements with the audience looking at you (not the screen), standing centre stage.

… in person

All Business Plans are presented in person. Maybe to a group using PowerPoint, maybe talking around a table, maybe just one-to-one in the bank to a junior manager. Whatever the situation, the point is the same; they will be buying into *you* as well as your Business Plan.

So some basic principles apply:

- Dress smartly.

  - If in doubt, wear a navy suit.

  - Keeping your jacket on is appropriate but if it is warm, take it off (better this than gently perspiring into a heap).

  - You want their money – look like the sort of person that you would lend money to.

- Be early. You'll be more in control.

- Be early. If you are on time now, they may be more likely to think you will not be late in your loan payments.

- Be enthusiastic.
- Know your Business Plan very well – you'll appear in control.
- Answer questions directly. You have nothing to hide.
- Have a copy of your Plan and a copy for each lender.
- Be confident but not arrogant.
- Believe in your Business Plan – you know it makes sense or else you wouldn't have come this far.
- Remember, they are buying *you* as much as your Plan.
- Think of this not as a pitch but as a conversation. Banks need companies to lend to in order to make their money as that is their business (although it doesn't mean they will every time).
- Having a conversation means you get lots of good feedback about your Business Plan.

Final point

Ahem … I have a confession to make. And I know it is very late to say it here but if I'd told you earlier you wouldn't have read this far (bit like a Business Plan really!). There is no guarantee that this Business Plan will work. Put simply, if there were a guaranteed Business Plan recipe everyone would be using it by now and all businesses would be working successfully.

'No plan survives contact with the enemy.'

Paraphrased: Helmuth von Moltke the Elder, 1800–1889,
Prussian Commander

There are too many variables in planning and running a business. Even, for example, different bank managers can take different views about a Business Plan. I remember listening to one quite famous entrepreneur: it was the twentieth bank they approached that lent them the money to get started. Overcoming all these variables will be constantly in your thoughts but the tenacity required to start your business will make it a success. Whilst this book will not give you a Business Plan that guarantees a profitable, sound business, the alternative isn't so attractive: no Business Plan, no business. Any Business Plan is a good start ...

> the tenacity required to start your business will make it a success

A key point, reflecting an earlier comment, is that a Business Plan is always a work in progress. So whenever you show or present it to someone and they respond negatively, ask them, 'What is it about my Plan you don't like?' It may be a little difficult to hear or to take at first, but this feedback is critical in developing your Plan and developing your business.

 **brilliant** recap

- Clarity is key. Really good ideas are easy to explain.
- Ask trusted people to review the contents of your Business Plan.
- Present it well on paper – even if it costs a few pounds.
- In person it is *you* lenders want to hear and see – the PowerPoint is a helpful means of illustrating detailed points. Be enthusiastic – by getting this far you know it is a good business.
- There is no guaranteed Business Plan. But no Business Plan is guaranteed to be a bad start.

CHAPTER 11

Your Business Plan in action

'A good plan, violently executed now, is better than a perfect plan next week.'

George S. Patton US general (1885–1945)

You are driving along a motorway and you know you need to exit at Junction 12. After a few minutes you see the sign for your junction, and you turn off. After a short distance what do you see on the left-hand side of the road? A sign? What does the sign say?

It has the number of the road you are now driving along. Why? It is there to reassure you that you are on the right road. That at the last junction you took the right road. And that same reassurance is one of the things your Business Plan gives you once the business is up and running.

Your Business Plan as a management tool

Once we are up and running our business plan has a number of other functions, including:

- Monitoring performance against targets.
- Helping to set budgets.
- Managing staff.

We know our Business Plan has a desirable future position at a given point in time (otherwise we wouldn't have started the business). Say we are in a good position at one month. And within the Plan we prepared a monthly income and expenditure account and a monthly cash-flow forecast. So at the end of Month 1, we will have:

- Predicted income in Month 1 (likely sales).
- Predicted expenditure in Month 1.
- Predicted cash-flow in Month 1.

Now at the end of Month 1 we can measure our:

- Exact income for Month 1.
- Exact expenditure Month 1.
- Exact cash-flow position for Month 1.

And we can compare these figures to establish if we are on target for Month 1 in all of these areas. If the answer is yes, first, congratulations, and secondly, this gives us reassurance about the future. If we were right about Month 1 then there is some confidence that we will be right about Months 2, 3, etc. And if we are right about the first three months then we can again have some belief that we are on the right road to Month 12. Don't look at each month alone: keep an 'accumulative total' to ensure we are not accumulating several small monthly losses into a big loss.

Signs of danger ...

What happens if our Month 1 figures are significantly different to the Plan? And the obvious 'significantly different' here is that

> trouble will occur, but it does require our immediate attention

they are worse, so income lower than expected, expenditure higher than expected or 'the big one', both at the same time.

Potentially we have trouble. In itself that isn't a problem as trouble will occur and one of our roles as business leader is to sort it out, but it does require our immediate attention. Two courses of action are needed:

- Look for the reason why.
- Run an updated profit and loss forecast and a cash-flow to see how significant the trouble is.

Are the reasons one-offs? Perhaps we underestimated how much the website would be or the vehicle fleet fuel bills are noticeably higher. Are these reasons likely to continue? Or are sales significantly down? And will they continue on a downward trend?

Deciding significance is clearly critical here and this is where the Business Plan is particularly helpful in that we can determine if we will run out of money. With the new figures we must update our cash-flow forecast and look at where we will be over the next 12 months. Will we run out of money? If no, we can survive, but we will have to make some changes (although not necessarily major ones). If yes, then immediate significant action is required. Best is to make some changes, e.g. increase sales or decrease costs, as these are more permanent solutions. A temporary answer is to arrange some short-term borrowing, e.g. an overdraft. Temporary, because an overdraft is going to cost us money, and we are in this position as our money situation is not as good as expected, so this is a reluctant choice. It is also worth reflecting that if we have any borrowings it was on the basis of the figures in our Business Plan, so if they are worse that may begin to affect our ability to borrow money. A worst-case scenario is our lender disliking our downturn so much that they demand repayment of our borrowings.

In the short term it is always easier to improve our financial position by cutting costs. The simple reason for this is shown below.

- If we cut £10,000 from costs, we make £10,000 more profit (in simple terms) as income − expenditure = profit.

- If we want to make £10,000 more profit by selling more, how much more do we need to sell? It depends on our profit margin, but it is NOT £10,000. We sell things but it costs us money to make those things and so our £10,000 needs to come from the profit margin, e.g. if we achieve a 25% profit margin we need to sell £40,000 of product/ services to make £10,000 of profit.

Of course it is perfectly possible to increase sales but usually this takes time and effort and sometimes we need an immediate increase in financial performance, so as business owners cutting costs often comes first. But we have to remember that we have to spend money to make money, and we have to be careful how we cut. If we remove a key member of staff it may save money short term but lose us money longer term. If we remove our marketing budget we may lose sales almost immediately.

 **tip**

Cutting costs is a valid strategy and it is quick, but we have to wield the knife carefully.

There is an alternative situation; our income is more, and/or our spending is less and our profit is more. What a marvellous position to be in. And it truly is marvellous, so why am I sounding like the voice of doom? Because it is possible to have too much business, and especially at the beginning we don't want our emerging reputation to be tarnished by failing to deliver or providing poor quality goods/services.

First, is it a temporary or permanent effect? If temporary we may be able to muddle through. If more permanent, perhaps we were too cautious in our Business Plan (not a bad thing to be) or our instincts about a growing market were right and it is just bigger than we expected. If so, we can re-evaluate our Business Plan and actions we might consider taking include:

- Increasing our resources, e.g. more staff.
- Increasing our prices to curb demand (and increase income).
- Delaying new product introductions

Helping to set budgets

This question of where to make cuts is part of the ongoing issue of where we deploy our money to best effect. And not just cuts; where do we spend more? Do we spend less or more on marketing, do we spend less or more on people in the factory?

When we wrote the Plan, we had to guess (to an extent) where we would spend our money. Now we are up and running we have more evidence to support our decisions. For example, we know better how much things are costing and what effect they have so, e.g., our advertising in the local newspaper has generated X number of sales, etc. This information is vital in helping to review our business so that it can become most effective.

> now we are up and running we have more evidence to support our decisions

Now that we can revisit our Plan and make adjustments to our budgets, what has to go up? What needs to go down? Can we only increase some things at the expense of others being cut? Using our income & expenditure and our cash-flow records we can make these decisions and assess their impact. This then allows us to set better budgets for the next quarter, year, etc.

Managing staff

One thing we notice when we run our business is there is often a difference between the owners and the employees. And as managers we may get frustrated when staff don't see things the way we do, perhaps not appearing to understand the position the firm is in. Not surprising, really, as we live and breathe the business, wrote the plan, we use the Business Plan in helping our decisions. For example, if we are dropping below our targets, then we have to up our game; if securing certain new clients is important for our reputation, then it is our responsibility. But our staff have not benefited from all our thinking and don't necessarily feel the same involvement in the business.

But if the staff saw the Business Plan, or were part of creating/updating it, then things might be better understood. If our delaying the purchase of a new machine/car is to navigate us around a cash-flow problem, then if the staff saw the figures in the Plan, they would understand more, would be less likely to kick against the decision, and be more willing to support it. If they saw in the Plan where the business is going and the targets it is setting then they may feel more committed to achieving those targets.

Sharing the Business Plan can be a tough thing to do for some people. Some are culturally disposed to having a clear gap between managers and workers and for others it requires opening up more than they are used to. But involving all our people in the Business Plan will increase understanding, and often help to write a better one in the first place.

What happens if the Plan is wrong ...?

As mentioned above, when we wrote our Business Plan we had to guess to an extent. Now because we have put a lot into researching and writing the Plan, it should generally be right. Not perfect, but no Business Plan ever is. But it should be at least ok. It is possible that despite all our good preparation the business just doesn't work as well as it was planned to. Reasons for this include the following:

- The market just doesn't respond as expected.

- We are too early into the market. Remember, we sought to make our products/services new, unique and innovative, and sometimes take-up of the new isn't as fast as expected.

- Sometimes we are too late. Perhaps getting the Plan into action was unexpectedly delayed.

- A competitor may respond to our entry in a different way to what we expected.

- Something beyond our control happens, e.g. I know someone who bought two fishing boats specifically to catch cod and then new government legislation reduced the amount of cod allowed to be caught.

We have three options:

1 Keep going in the belief that, for example, the market will change.

2 Seriously change what the business does.

3 Shut down the business (and start another one).

There is no easy way to call this one as the context is always different. Once we have been in business a while our senses become more attuned and we develop an instinct for which way to go. But even from the start of our operation, we will develop these senses. There are two additional aspects to consider in making our decisions:

> our senses become more attuned and we develop an instinct for which way to go

1 Remember that change costs time, effort and money. If we leave it too late, until we have run out of money, we won't be able to alter anything. It is therefore important to change whilst we continue to have some resources to do so.

2 Is your home at risk? If not, then you have more freedom to make decisions and you have the option to 'tough it

out'. If it is at risk through being used in security for your business finance, that changes things. Taking risks is good in starting a business; taking stupid risks is just that, stupid. A personal view: it is a lot nicer to write the Business Plan for your next business from the comfort of your home.

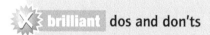 **dos and don'ts**

Do

✔ Address the situation early, don't ignore it.

What next?

Your Business Plan brought your business into reality. And it guided you through the early months. Therefore it is useful and you should stay with it as you develop your business.

- Use it to guide your month-to-month decisions.
- As time goes by the Business Plan needs to be continually extended to coincide with the next month, quarter, year, etc.
- It reminds us what we are all doing.

But along with the incremental development of our Business Plan, we do need to have larger scale reviews. Just as in the beginning we reviewed the external/internal environment, to achieve some match between what the world needs and what we want to offer, we need to do that again. The development of the world or our business is not a smooth, linear path. It tends to happen in steps, e.g. new economies, new legislation, new competitors, etc., so it is therefore important to review our Plan to keep us in touch with global developoments.

'A life spent making mistakes is not only more honorable, but more useful than a life spent doing nothing.'

George Bernard Shaw, Irish dramatist and socialist (1856–1950)

... and some final thoughts

Don't	Do
Try and trick the tax people.	Get a good accountant (and other professional advisers).
Assume a market exists just because you want to do something you like.	Some proper market research to prove the market exists.
Assume your products/services will just sell themselves.	Identify a real sustainable competitive advantage.
Get sucked into the business so you cannot see the wood for the trees.	Be that complex person who loves their business but can still think about it objectively.
Cut short your planning so you feel uncertain.	Believe in your Business Plan.
Throw everything you have at the business.	Keep a financial lifeboat.
Go into business come what may.	Remember that if, through the planning, you prove this isn't a good business idea, move on, there will be another idea somewhere.
Give up.	Remember that if you have come this far, there will be an opportunity somewhere.

Appendices

Appendix 1 – Business Plan template

This is a Business Plan for

XXXXXXXXXXXXXXXXXXXX

Presented by

XXXXXXXXXXXXXXXXXXXXXXXXXXXXXX

Dated:

Contact details: Name: xxxxxxxx

                           Telephone: xxxxxxxx

                           Email: xxxxxxxx

Executive Summary
For guidance see Chapter 9.

In writing the Executive Summary we need to address five key questions:

1. *Is there a market?*
2. *Does the business have the products/services to win?*
3. *Does the business have the people to make it happen?*
4. *How much money will the business make?*
5. *Where will the business go?*

Description of the Business
For guidance see Chapter 3 and address the specific Business Plan Actions.

See also BUSINESS PLAN ACTION: Write a short statement (say 30 words max.) that makes it clear what your business is and what it does.

Our Mission
For guidance see Chapter 3 and address the specific Business Plan Actions.

See also BUSINESS PLAN ACTION: Write your Mission Statement (say 30 words max.) that makes it clear what your purpose is.

Our Vision
For guidance see Chapter 3 and address the specific Business Plan Actions.

See also BUSINESS PLAN ACTION: Present your Vision (say 30 words max.) that makes it clear what your purpose is.

<u>What we do</u>
For guidance see Chapter 3 and address the specific Business Plan Actions.

See also BUSINESS PLAN ACTION: Present a summary of your day-to-day activities and particularly what you will do for customers and what you will do in your operations.

<u>Our Values and Guiding Principles</u>
For guidance see Chapter 3 and address the specific Business Plan Actions.

See also BUSINESS PLAN ACTION: If you wish to present a short statement on the values of your business, this would be a good place to do it as part of this Business Plan section that describes your business. You may then wish to define a set of guiding principles.

<u>Our Competitive Position</u>
For guidance see Chapter 4 and address the specific Business Plan Actions.

In the Business Plan you should provide summaries of the main thrust of your competitive position, e.g.:

- See BUSINESS PLAN ACTION: Which of the generic strategies will you pursue? (One paragraph.) Explain why you are making this choice (two to three paragraphs), supporting your arguments with numbers. Map your business and your competitors' on the basis of their competitive strategy (cost leader, differentiation, focus) to reveal the gap you will occupy.

- See BUSINESS PLAN ACTION: How will you build sustainability (business, not green) into your Business Plan? Spend two to three paragraphs explaining why your business will have a future.

- BUSINESS PLAN ACTION: Present a summary of your PESTLE analysis to highlight the key issues that, in the future, will provide opportunities for your business and that are threats. Include a copy of your full PESTLE analysis in the appendices to your Business Plan.

- BUSINESS PLAN ACTION: Present a summary of your Porter's 5 Forces analysis to highlight that it shows the (current and future) degree of competition in your chosen industry/market, and what factors make it attractive for your business to enter.

- BUSINESS PLAN ACTION: Present a summary of your SWOT to highlight you are aware of the realism of your position, i.e. strengths and weaknesses, opportunities and threats. Show how you will use your strengths to address these opportunities, threats and weaknesses.

Our Marketing
For guidance see Chapter 4 and address the specific Business Plan Actions.

In the Business Plan you should present your marketing plans, e.g.:

- BUSINESS PLAN ACTION: Give a summary of your marketing and sales strategy and activity.

- BUSINESS PLAN ACTION: Present your (i) strategic marketing and (ii) promotional marketing plans.

- BUSINESS PLAN ACTION: Define very clearly and precisely the 'want' or 'need' your business is addressing (remember, a business will only survive if it addresses a real need).

- BUSINESS PLAN ACTION: State what products you will sell. Make some comment on how you will maintain the price margins vs those of internet retailers. Or become an internet retailer. Or say how you will move your products to become a service. Or if you will sell a service (see later section), say what services you will be selling.

- If your are selling products – BUSINESS PLAN ACTION: Answer this question: What will be the three main reasons that will bring customers into my premises to try my products?

- If you are selling services – BUSINESS PLAN ACTION: List and briefly explain the factors that you will use to make your service viable, e.g.:

  - Who will market/sell the service?

  - What makes them right for the task?

  - What guarantees will you offer customers?

  - What testimonials will you provide?

  - Do you have or can you get references from customers?

- BUSINESS PLAN ACTION: Which markets will you be in? Why?

- BUISNESS PLAN ACTION: What will be your approach to your chosen market(s)?

- BUSINESS PLAN ACTION: List the three main ways you want your business to be perceived. And how will you communicate these messages?

- Naming your business – BUSINESS PLAN ACTION:

  - Write the name of your business.

- Give a one sentence reason for choosing it.

- Give the domain name you have bought/registered.

- Our chosen customers – BUSINESS PLAN ACTION: Describe your target customers in as much detail as possible.

- Our chosen customers – BUSINESS PLAN ACTION: Do market research by asking target customers about their existing product/supplier/offer. Present your findings, to help demonstrate there is a need for your products/services/company.

- How Big is your Market? Present the results of your research and calculations to describe the size of your chosen market. Show, with information, if it is growing, staying the same, or declining.

- Pricing – describe how and why you set your prices.

  - BUSINESS PLAN ACTION: What is the price range present in your chosen market?

  - BUSINESS PLAN ACTION: Decide on your pricing strategy.

  - BUSINESS PLAN ACTION: Will you discount? If so, what will be your discount policy?

  - BUSINESS PLAN ACTION: Give your prices for your initial products and services. Show your profit margins at these prices.

- BUSINESS PLAN ACTION: What sort of website will you have? Give reasons for your choice. Allocate some costs.

Financial Considerations

- BUSINESS PLAN ACTION: Write a statement, no numbers, about how your business will make money. Make it short, make it clear, as nothing interests people more than a precise answer to the question: 'How will this business make money?'

- BUSINESS PLAN ACTION: How will you manage your cash-flow? It is very important to put this in your Business Plan as getting it wrong will lead your business to an early death.

Funding the Business

- BUSINESS PLAN ACTION: Present (i) a full description of how your business will be funded; and (ii) show this funding in your Profit & Loss, cash-flow forecasts and balance sheet.

Our people

- BUSINESS PLAN ACTION: Compile evidence of your experience in being a manager and/or leader. Present reasons why you will adjust to the position of being the boss. Show how you will spend your time.

- BUSINESS PLAN ACTION: Show how you will ensure the key activities are adequately covered. Include specific people, with their backgrounds, to demonstrate to yourself and lenders/investors that you have the right people and you will make the right team.

- BUSINESS PLAN ACTION: Present your plans for growth (or otherwise). Give the reader a clear impression on how big you will be and how quickly you plan to get there. Add how you plan to grow.

- BUSINESS PLAN ACTION: If you are to be a family business, write a short piece (one paragraph) to highlight the issues you may encounter and what actions you are taking to mitigate these issues.

Protecting our Knowledge

- BUSINESS PLAN ACTION: Do a knowledge audit of your proposed business, i.e. what knowledge do you or will you possess in your business that is particularly valuable or even critical to your business?

- BUSINESS PLAN ACTION: How will you protect your knowledge and stop your business losing critical knowledge? What steps can you take to mitigate the loss of such key people/knowledge?

  - Include some statements about knowledge. What is the important/critical knowledge?

  - Explain how you will protect certain knowledge embedded in your business, e.g. through relationships.

  - If you business is based upon Intellectual Property rights, and especially if you are seeking external investment, you must have a very clear presentation of it and all the technical/legal details.

Appendix 2 – Illustrative Business Plan templates

Business Plans don't change in their fundamental nature and whatever the business, addressing the same key questions is a common theme, e.g. what is the market need? Are the right people in place? How much money will it make? All the common parts of the Business Plan remain.

However, different types of business do require a change of emphasis between the sections of the report and in particular certain sections become more important. Below are some examples of this change of emphasis within the standard Business Plan template.

<u>Template – for a Hotel Business</u>

Background:	Planning a new hotel business that will take over an existing hotel premises.
Primary Business Plan sections:	Location and nature of the premises.
Secondary sections:	Marketing (customer segmentation).
	Staffing and service.

We can change many things with a hotel business: rebrand it, change its market position, redecorate, even potentially extend it. But the one thing we cannot do is change its location. And it is easy to see that the location of a hotel has a big impact. For example, a hotel near a tourist beauty spot will have an obvious potential audience; a hotel near an airport will have an obvious target customer group. But what of the hotel that used to have a main road passing it but which is now diverted?

Modifications required to the standard Business Plan:

What is my business?	Place a greater emphasis on explaining the location of this hotel. What factors make it a good location? For what reasons? Why would people be in the area and what reason would they want to stay? Is it primarily a business hotel or a leisure hotel? Is it the right size for

	your purpose, e.g. a hotel with 60+ rooms that can take coach parties? A hotel near a major airport may need to have 24hr service, etc.
Beating the competition	Will you be the only hotel in the area? On what basis will you beat the competitors? If you were to draw up a list of hotels in the area based on their relative attractiveness to customers, where would you rank? Is this high enough to get sufficient business?
Marketing	Who are your core target customers? Businesspeople, leisure users, families, retired people? Whichever target group it is, do you have a compelling offering for it? How will you fill it with business in off-peak times, e.g. a business hotel is relatively empty on Saturday and Sunday, so what will you do with no core customer group? A 'wedding hotel' doesn't do much during the week.

People?	Can you hire and retain staff with the right service skills? An away-from-it-all location may be idyllic, but can you get sufficiently good staff to work there?
Related business types:	Other service businesses that require customers to visit them, e.g. pubs, restaurants, sandwich bars, shops, etc. will also have a very strong location dimension to their Business Plan.

Template – for a Consulting Business

Background:	You and a colleague leaving the company to start your own consulting business.
Primary Business Plan sections:	People.
Secondary sections:	Knowledge.

A consulting business is a classic professional services business and is about service quality. There are specifically two key areas to address: relationships and knowledge.

Modifications required to the standard business plan:

People	Key to a successful consulting business is the people. How good are their customer relationships? How

good are they in initiating contact and maintaining and delighting customers? Remembering this is a classic 'service' business and customers judge the quality of the service by the person selling/delivering it to them. Knowledge is also important but arguably a consultant with superior relationship skills and less knowledge may do better than one with all the knowledge and poor relationship skills. Are there established customer relationships that will form the basis of initial assignments and income? How will the business grow? Is it scalable?

Knowledge

But of course knowledge is very important – it is often why firms call in a consultant. Emphasise scale of knowledge held relevant to the key markets for the new business. Highlight how knowledge will be updated.

Related business types:

Any professional services-type businesses, e.g.

law firms, accountants, architects, etc.

<u>Template – for a Fashion Business</u>

Background: You will establish a business designing, manufacturing and selling a new range of clothes.

Primary Business Plan sections: Marketing.

Secondary sections: Operations.

Unless we are going to sell non-branded clothes (almost certainly a cost leadership model of business), fashion is about brand. It is about brand and its relationship to its chosen customer group. And that customer group is often very narrow and needs to be very well defined. What often scares lenders about creative businesses is that the owners get very enthusiastic about the creative side but lack focus on the operational side, e.g. getting the clothes made, getting them into shops on time (they are fashion, after all) and getting the money in! So operations need to be emphasised.

Modifications required to the standard Business Plan:

Marketing It is very difficult to have a fashion brand that appeals to all customer groups, so strategic marketing and, specifically, defining the core customer group is critical. In doing so we get to know what they like, think, how they communicate, spend, etc. very closely and we can ensure we achieve a brand fit between us and this chosen group. Development of our brand will likely be a key source of competitive advantage and how this will happen needs to be well specified, including how it will differ from other brands in the market.

People/operations

Several operational dimensions are important here and need to be well considered and presented:

Where will the clothes be made? Is there anything special about the production process (e.g. made in home country)? Or if not, likely they will be made overseas to harness lower cost of production. If so, how will you control this process, ensuring delivery deadlines, quality control, etc? Will they be made at home or overseas? Overseas may be cheaper but shipping the products may take weeks – is that fast enough for a

	'fashion' business? How will you sell the clothes? Your shops (back to shop location) or other people's shops? If others', how will you get them to stock your clothes? What sort of relationships do you have with key retailers?
Related business types	Other fashion businesses, e.g. jewellery, upmarket goods such as watches, etc.

<u>Template – for a Manufacturing Business in B2B markets</u>

Background:	You will make products for use by other companies.
Primary Business Plan sections:	Operations.
Secondary sections:	People/relationships.

Companies as customers are less emotional and more objectives about products than high-street consumers. Companies understand time is money so the cost of failure of the component or late delivery is very significant, maybe even critical for them. Cost is always important.

Modifications required to the standard Business Plan:

People/operations	Your customers have factories to make their products. These factories cannot work unless they have a regular and constant

supply of raw materials. So your failing to deliver could cost them a fortune if their factory is idle and their workers are standing around with nothing to do. Equally, if our component fails, their product fails. Again this costs them a fortune and damages their reputation. So in our Business Plan we must emphasise and demonstrate our operational efficiency, our quality systems and our ability to produce acceptable quality at an acceptable price.

Marketing/relationships

In a B2C market we might have thousands, even millions of customers. In a B2B market we might have hundreds or even tens of customers. So if we upset customers, where do we go for new ones? Our ability to have excellent customer relationships, even when we have problems, is critical to our Business Plan and how we address this needs to be a key part of the Plan, e.g. industry experience/

| | reputation/relationships with key individuals, etc. |
| Related business types | Any B2B market-based businesses. |

Appendix 3 – PESTLE analysis

PESTLE analysis is a tool to help us understand the big things that happen. These 'big things' or 'macroeconomic factors' are things like an economic recession, or an aging population, that no one business can change. Instead we seek to identify them, hopefully ahead of them happening, and then change our business to ensure we are in a good position to 'survive' them or to make the most of the opportunity presented by the changes.

For example, an economic recession means most businesses will suffer a fall in sales so if we know this is going to happen we can change our business (e.g. cut costs) or perhaps even sell it. However, in a recession people may not stop spending but may spend on cheaper things. So knowing a recession is on its way gives us a good opportunity to introduce lower-cost ranges of products.

To do a PESTLE analysis you will need to spend time researching the changes in big things in the next five years or so. Look to find three to five key changes under each heading that could impact upon your area of business. Include numbers to give scale, i.e. saying 'the number of older people is increasing' is good. But saying the number of those over 80 will increase by 2% p.a. for the next ten years is much more helpful.

Political: Factors that originate from national governments, including other government organisations. Examples include new laws, new policies and new proposals.

Economic: Under this heading put things such as interest changes, economic growth, recessions, etc.

Social: This heading is for changes in society, be it physical, i.e. population growth, change, education policies, but also cultural, i.e. changing beliefs, etc.

Technological: Changes in technology that facilitate new things, e.g. the internet, but also make some technology obsolete, e.g. CDs replaced by MP3 and USB storage devices.

Legal: Changes in law.

Environmental: Changes in law, attitudes toward the environment.

Note: Sometimes a given item could fit in one or more category; it doesn't really matter which one it goes in, as long as it is there.

Then list the key findings from this macroeconomic analysis as they impact upon your proposed business.

Appendix 4 – Porter's 5 Forces analysis

The PESTLE analysis is a tool to look at the big things in life and these will affect all markets (for markets also read industries). For example, a rise in interest rates will impact upon all companies across all markets. Having said that, not all markets may be affected to the same extent, e.g. a rise in interest rates may affect the housing industry more than the food industry (as higher interest rates affect both company debt and consumer spending). In our Business Plan we need to analyse the industry/market that our business works within to ensure we know how that market works. To do this we can use a tool called Porter's 5 Forces (P5F) as it helps us understand a number of things, but particularly it highlights competition and balance of power.

Doing a P5F analysis is similar to doing a PESTLE analysis, i.e., you will need to spend time researching how the industry works now and in the next five years or so. Look to find three to five key issues under each heading that could impact upon your area of business. Again, include numbers to give scale.

Potential entrants: How easy is it to set up in this industry? Is it easy or does it take a lot of resources? If it is easy, and you do a good job, lots of other firms will follow you, thereby increasing competition. If it is difficult to enter and establish yourself, it will be harder for you but also harder for others. Is it a brand-driven industry? If so, you will need to build a brand to enter.

Potential substitutes: How easy is it to switch to another type of product or service? This isn't just direct competitors but substitutes, e.g. you may be launching a new brand of cola so other brands of cola are direct competitors. But people drink cola to quench thirst. So cola can be substituted not only by lemonade, but also fruit juice, water, etc.

Power of suppliers: This is about the relative balance of power between you and the suppliers. Two much supplier power makes the market unattractive. How easy is it for you to switch suppliers? Easy is good, difficult means they have more power over you.

Power of buyers: This is the other side, and is between you and the customers. How easy is it for them to switch away from you? If it is easy they have a lot of power and you will have to work hard to keep their loyalty. Is this industry/market sufficiently attractive to you? If

	it is difficult to switch then that becomes attractive. Consider supermarkets where it is very easy for customers to start shopping at another one versus personal computer operating systems, where it is very difficult for people to switch.
Competitive rivalry:	How many competitors are there in this market? Many? Few? Importantly, is there enough business for all the competitors? If the market is growing then even if there are a lot of competitors there may be enough business for everyone. If the market is shrinking then not everyone will survive, so it is an attractive market.

This all adds up to an assessment of the attractiveness of the marketplace. There is no point in going to all the trouble of setting up a business in an unattractive market that will probably mean you will struggle to make money and may have a limited life. Better to pick an attractive market.

Appendix 5 – Sources of information and support

There are many sources of information available and some are given below. Some are free and some charge. Why not start with the free ones and then if you have identified any gaps in your knowledge/support, look to buy-in support as you need it.

Government support

- Most governments positively encourage people to start their own businesses (especially as traditional industries decline and other work moves abroad) and frequently they provide support to those embarking on this journey. Look at:
  - National government – in the UK Business Link is a national service to help new businesses and those planning them.
  - Local government – many local enterprise agencies support and encourage people to start their own businesses. Some local authorities also have small grants available to start-ups.
  - The tax authorities in your country may often publish useful guidance books, notes, etc.

Chambers of commerce

These exist in many countries and they may be able to help in providing you with information on support, making introductions and running events. Events with other businesspeople are worth attending as in conversation you can ask about accountants, etc. Best not to go with the first accountant or lawyer, etc. you meet or are recommended but wait, ask a number of businesspeople, and see if any names are continually recommended.

Professional associations

Professional associations exist for all professionals, e.g.

accountants, lawyers, intellectual property lawyers, food safety consultants, health and safety advisers, etc. Contact them nationally or locally and ask what they can offer by way of support, introductions, etc.

Trade associations

Such associations exist in many industries and attending their events could be useful – it will give you a chance to look at the opposition!

Membership organisations

- Groups such as the Federation of Small Businesses often give support as part of their membership.
- Many local marketing groups work together to promote business in certain areas and/or in specific industries.
- Many local networking groups exist and hold regular meetings where good speakers share their experience. One can meet other businesspeople with potential business opportunities or just share/ talk about experiences as a fellow business owner.

Universities and business schools

Frequently universities and business schools have students who are looking for opportunities as part of their course or internships, and for little or no money they may be able to provide you with some resources as part of your planning or when you are up and running.

Get a mentor

A mentor may have different roles; they can be a

sounding-board or critical friend for you to test your ideas and thinking upon. They can be someone with industry knowledge and/or they can be someone with good contacts that they will introduce you to. You may be able to pay someone to be a mentor but local programmes exist that pair mentors with businesses. In this case the mentors are often retired or semi-retired and they find it interesting to be involved with your business and share their knowledge/experience.

Index

the brilliant series

Fast and engaging, the *Brilliant* series works hard to make sure you stand out from the crowd. Each *Brilliant* book has been carefully crafted to ensure everything you read is practical and applicable – to help you make a difference now.

9780273722328

9780273720591

9780273717355

9780273743217

9780273726463

9780273725114

9780273721239

9780273712350

9780273734147

9780273714804

9780273730675

9780273730910

9780273720799

9780273727347

9780273721826

9780273738077

9780273737452

9780273742555

9780273744092

9780273724902

9780273732556

9780273740544

9780273735885

9780273723271

Whatever your level, we'll get you to the next one. It's all about you. Get ready to shine!

Prentice Hall
is an imprint of